UNITY and DIFFERENCE IN AMERICAN LIFE

RELIGION AND CIVILIZATION SERIES

RELIGION AND THE WORLD ORDER

WORLD ORDER: ITS INTELLECTUAL AND CULTURAL FOUNDATIONS

FOUNDATIONS OF DEMOCRACY

F. Ernest Johnson, *Editor*

GROUP RELATIONS AND GROUP ANTAGONISMS

CIVILIZATION AND GROUP RELATIONSHIPS

UNITY AND DIFFERENCE IN AMERICAN LIFE

R. M. MacIver, *Editor*

FORTHCOMING VOLUMES

WELLSPRINGS OF THE AMERICAN SPIRIT

F. Ernest Johnson, *Editor*

LABOR LOOKS AHEAD

Liston Pope, *Editor*

GENERAL EDITORIAL BOARD

Louis Finkelstein

F. Ernest Johnson   R. M. MacIver

George N. Shuster

RELIGION AND CIVILIZATION SERIES

UNITY and DIFFERENCE IN AMERICAN LIFE

A series of addresses and discussions

EDITED BY

R. M. MacIver

Published by

INSTITUTE FOR RELIGIOUS & SOCIAL STUDIES

Distributed by

HARPER & BROTHERS

NEW YORK AND LONDON

PRINTED IN THE UNITED STATES OF AMERICA
BY THE VAIL-BALLOU PRESS, INC., BINGHAMTON, N. Y.

To
ALVIN JOHNSON

CONTENTS

PART ONE

THE COMMON GROUND

I. Three Paths to the Common Good   *Louis Finkelstein*   5

II. The Rise of an American Culture   *Allan Nevins*   15

III. What Common Ground Has America Won?   *Lawrence K. Frank*   33

PART TWO

THE DIVIDING ISSUES

IV. The Racial Issue   *E. Franklin Frazier*   43

V. The Ethnic Issue   *Vilhjalmur Stefansson*   61

VI. The Economic Issue   *Eli Ginzberg*   77

VII. The Religious Issue   *Ralph W. Sockman*   89

PART THREE

WHAT WE CAN DO ABOUT THEM

VIII. What the Schools Can Do   *Clyde R. Miller*   107

IX. What the Press Can Do   *Gerald W. Johnson*   119

X. What Business Can Do   *Edward L. Bernays*   131

XI. What the Courts Can Do   *Walton Hale Hamilton*   143

XII. What We All Can Do   *R. M. MacIver*   151

Contributors   159

Index   163

PART ONE

THE COMMON GROUND

I

INTRODUCTORY STATEMENT BY THE EDITOR

Three years ago, the Institute for Religious Studies, under the guidance of Doctor Finkelstein, inaugurated a series of addresses on Group Relations. It was an attempt to get together men of scholarship and men of understanding to explore and to expound one of the main issues that face our modern society. It was one of the very first attempts of the kind.

The first of these series has resulted in the publication of a volume on *Group Relations and Group Antagonisms*. The second volume of the series has as its title *Civilization and Group Relationships*. This book presents the contributions of the third series. This time we are approaching the subject from a somewhat different standpoint. We are thinking of the relation between the multitude of groups among us and the unity of America, the national unity as it is affected by our group differences and our group divisions.

Many things have changed since this course was started two years ago. The most bitter and bigoted enemy of group harmony has been totally vanquished. But that has by no means ended this struggle. Even those who fought in the name of a more liberal world, a more understanding world, may be in some degree infected by this virus. The struggle is on, and it will not end in any total surrender. It will continue because it goes deep into the problems of our human nature. What we look for is betterment, improvement of relationships; what we work for is the victory of one side in the struggle, but we cannot hope for the total surrender of the other side.

Recently the subject to which we have been devoted has been receiving increased attention. People have become much more aware that there is here a vital problem for America. On the one hand we have a greater awareness of the problem. You see it, for example, in the number of organizations that now are beginning to promote studies in this field. At the same time there has also been—at least there is evidence of—an increase in the very thing these organizations exist to combat, an increase in group intolerance, an increase in the strength of prejudice throughout the country. Both sides are marshaled; the fight is on.

In this fight we have two kinds of weapons and both must be used. We have spiritual weapons and we have scientific weapons. When I speak about the spiritual weapons, I mean the understanding, and the source of the understanding, that make men think in terms of brotherhood and of good will among men and all that lies back of that.

When I speak of scientific weapons, I mean the advancement and the effective presentation of the truth regarding groups and group relationships and of the consequences of group divisions on the national unity and the national welfare. It is curious that, although we live in a world where science is honored more than ever before and regarded as the ultimate arbiter of things, we absolutely refuse to be scientific when we are thinking of groups one against another, when we are looking at groups other than our own. In other words, we refuse to see these other groups as they are. We—the great majority of us, all of us in some degree—see other groups through a mist of prejudice and misunderstanding. That is a thing we have to combat. It is a long struggle, but, if we can bring out the issues, if we can show both the personal and the national loss that comes from taking the viewpoint of intolerance and prejudice, then we shall go a long way toward victory.

We lose personally and we lose nationally because of this prejudice. As people, as men and women, we lose because we narrow our understanding, the range of our experience, our whole life; because of it we close our minds as well as our hearts. Much of the richness of life is lost because of it. We lose above all the sense of the common, that which is universal in mankind and which therefore is the matrix of our being.

But we lose nationally, and here is the issue to which this series is devoted: We lose nationally because, of all nations, of all countries, ours depends more than any other on the cultivation of co-operativeness and good will between groups. Without that there is no such thing as an American way of life: without that it is very difficult to know that America stands for anything. It was for the development of that unity that this country came into being, to the sense of its own quality. In the growth of division, of separation and antagonism of groups we are faced with a national loss of momentous character.

—R. M. MacIver

THREE PATHS TO THE COMMON GOOD

BY

LOUIS FINKELSTEIN

I. THE BASIC PROBLEM

The problem of group relations in our country is basic to the survival of civilization. The moral influence of America is indispensable to the establishment of world understanding, and this influence can be exerted only if America sets its own moral house in order. American failure to overcome infringement of minority rights compromises our standing in the world, and makes our pleas for co-operation among men of different cultures seem hypocritical.

The problem of group relations will, I believe, not be solved merely by the introduction of new techniques of organization and education. It will require the reorientation of our people in three ways, interrelated and inherent in the religious traditions of the western world. They are the development of emphases on (a) the common interests of people as against their diverse interests; (b) long-range views as against short-range ones; (c) the spiritual aspects of life as against its material ones.

Any group or institution has two diverse types of interest. It has its group or institutional concerns, in which it regards itself as the rival or opponent of all other groups or institutions, particularly those close to it. Thus a trade union may regard its interests as opposed to those of the employer; the southern Negro has his quarrels with the southern white.

But the more thoughtful in each group will realize that beyond these divisive interests, there are centripetal ones, shared by opposing groups. The prosperity of an industry often has more effect on the lives of the employees and employers than the results of their struggles against one another. The prosperity and well-being of the South as a whole is more significant in the life of both whites and Negroes than is their relative position in the struggle for power.

The tendency of group and institutional organizations is to look away from the common ground and to concentrate on divisive and explosive issues. This is because the belligerent and aggressive impulses in us are far more effectively stimulated in our western culture than the impulses making for co-operation and understanding. Yet everywhere there is evidence that some men and women are beginning to appreciate the peril to all groups and institutions of democratic lands from emphasis on that which divides us rather than on that which unites us. We are beginning to realize that America's greatness is in large part due to the fact that we have overcome the tendency of sectional groups to regard their prosperity as deriving primarily from emphases on local advantage, and to substitute a tendency to recognize that prosperity is national. We must now extend the principle of national unity from the geographical to the social sphere, and from the national to the world sphere. We must train ourselves to realize that, while New York may gain some advantage in rivalry with some other state, its main opportunities for well-being derive from the hope that all will benefit. Similarly the advantage of all the various social groups within the United States—the religious groups, the racial groups, the economic groups, etc.—lies in common well-being far more than it does in rivalry and competition. So also the United States as a nation might gain at the expense of other peoples, but can be served far better through measures which are for the advantage of all.

This is an extremely difficult truth to inculcate. Even when we recognize it intellectually, we do not respond to it emotionally. The fact that a loan to Great Britain is an advantage to that country seems to the unwary reader of a hostile editorial sure proof that the measure is of disadvantage to our own. This conclusion is reached because from infancy we are reared with the primitive notion that in human relations one gains what the other loses, not realizing that usually both parties can gain at the same time. In the United States and other large federations the emotion of national patriotism has been substituted for local patriotism. Thus there has been some mitigation of the sectional tendency to regard the advantage of a neighbor as necessarily an evil for oneself. But our patriotism still tends to be geographical. We sing, "My country 'tis of thee"; and one of our great patriots spoke of "My country, may it always be right; but right or wrong, my country." We have extended the love of native locality to cover the whole land. But our sense of rivalry with those in the nations differing from us is still stronger than our sense of kinship with them. Beyond American boundaries we have developed no sense of "one world," either geographically or on a kinship basis.

Yet the sense of national unity, as opposed to group interest, and the sense of world unity as opposed to international rivalry must be developed, if humanity is to overcome the fearful trials which threaten us.

II. LONG-RANGE PLANNING

One of the ways in which we can overcome the divisive tendencies, both on a national and a world scale, is to think in long-range terms. Even those who fail to recognize the importance of the larger group from the viewpoint of immediate advantage cannot help recognizing that in the long run the broader the group whose well-being is considered, the more likely the development of advantage to all. For example, the immediate benefits to an employer from "victory" over a striking group of employees may be real. But if he is wise, he will consider whether similar "victories" by other employers (which may well be stimulated by his) will lead to a diminution of national purchasing power and, consequently, to a loss of trade far more disastrous than defeat in the particular labor struggle concerned. In other words, most "victories" in the struggles between groups (and even between nations) are Pyrrhic, when weighed by their effects over a sufficiently long span, the span even of a generation.

But thinking in terms of long periods is important not merely because it helps us overcome the tendency toward divisiveness; it is equally important because it is the only type of social thinking that can be really effective. The present is virtually determined by the conditions of the past. If man is free to mold his life, it is only in terms of the future. And the more distant the future, the more free he is to choose alternatives.

Thus in selecting a president of the United States—surely always a decision fraught with significant consequences to the nation and to the world—the freedom of choice on the part of the people of the United States becomes continually more limited as election day approaches. Even a year before election day, possible candidates for the office are limited in number to those who have already achieved recognition and have developed a taste for office. If we live in a generation when many of the best minds turn to industry rather than politics, the choice of candidates will be limited to men who are perhaps little above mediocrity. We may regret this situation; but there is little that we can do about it. The time to plan for effective presidents is not the year before a particular election day, but a generation before. We can train our children to the ideal of public service, to see in the discharge of high office an opportunity to help their fellow men. This will at once draw into public office men of real gifts, and will tend to make these men, when selected to office, better office-holders. But the effect of such inculcation will not be realized for many a year, when the children now in the primary grades attain the age fitting them for public service.

Similarly, the time to prevent bloody conflict is not on the eve of the outbreak of war, when a whole generation of misguided and mistaken policy has led inevitably to an impasse between nations. On December 7, 1941, America had virtually no alternative to war with the Axis. It is probable that its alternatives had actually been destroyed a number of years before. But certainly there was a time in the generation which preceded Pearl Harbor when war could have been avoided. Unfortunately, at each step in the long period between the wars, we were improvising in terms of the immediate situation, not looking ahead sufficiently to prevent ultimate catastrophe.

The tendency to court disaster by failing to look sufficiently far ahead is emphasized by the shortness of human life, and the even shorter terms of office for responsible positions. Hezekiah, warned by the far-seeing Prophet that the kings of Babylonia whom he was encouraging were destined to ruin Judea, replied naïvely, "Good is the word of the Lord which thou hast spoken . . . Is it not so, if peace and truth shall be in my days" (II Kings 20.19). Undoubtedly many leaders, perhaps less candid than Hezekiah, have steeled themselves against disaster, provided they felt certain it would not come in their own time.

One of the difficulties in planning the immediate future is that the nearer we approach a crisis, the smaller the difference between the alternatives still open. Issues which must be decided with a view to crises already upon us never take the form of white and black: they are always different shades of gray, and people cannot generally agree as to which is the lighter and which the darker shade. But in long-range planning, we are emotionally less affected, and at the same time the differences between the various policies are far more clear.

Some time ago, a group in the Conference on Science, Philosophy, and Religion—in fact, Professors Lyman Bryson, F. Ernest Johnson, R. M. MacIver, and I—worked out a questionnaire for about two hundred persons, asking what kind of world they would like to see emerge within twenty-five years. The unanimity in the replies was impressive and interesting. But how little unanimity there would have been in the same group, if our questionnaire had dealt with issues of tomorrow or the next day!

Sometimes we can appreciate large situations from the analogy of comparatively limited ones. The point I am making about the importance of long-range views in social thinking is illustrated, I believe, by my own experience as president of the Jewish Theological Seminary of America. It may be supposed that the chief executive officer of such an institution would exert a great influence on its immediate affairs. Actually there is little that a president of this Seminary can do to affect its decisions in his own time. The Seminary is today far more under the influence of my predecessors, Sabato Morais, Solomon Schechter, and Cyrus Adler, than my own. They chose the place where it is located; they selected most of the members of its present faculty; most of the alumni were trained by them, and they drew most of the lay Board of Directors into our work. In making these decisions, they set the pattern for the Seminary as it operates today. Whatever contribution I can make to the institution may become apparent a generation from now, when the men now being trained at the Seminary are its distinguished alumni, when new members of the faculty, now being selected, are its teachers, and when the laymen whom I may have influenced are guarding its material interests.

We utilize our gifts to the greatest advantage if we ourselves and our children have a vivid picture of the future, recognize that sufferings of the future generations will be as real as ours, and try to alleviate the ills of the body politic in the coming years. This fact must be stressed because we belong to an impatient generation with little time to think of the future, which cannot believe that there is little it can do to affect the disasters of the present. The best we can do with regard to the sufferings of the moment is to find palliatives; the therapies for human ills can be discovered only if we are willing to be patient and plan for a distant time.

Even the Prophets of Israel, inspired geniuses, were virtually without effect on the flux of events in their own time. Their effectiveness must be measured not in terms of the acceptance of their message by contemporaries, such as the Kings of Judah and Israel, but in the influence the Prophets may have exerted on future generations. Isaiah did not succeed in dissuading Ahaz from his disastrous foreign policy; but Isaiah has made a whole series of generations more keenly aware of the reality of the moral law and the reality of God.

III. THE SPIRITUAL LIFE

Perhaps the main reason we find it so difficult to think in terms of world needs and of the long-range future, is that for several generations we have been moving away from recognition of the importance of the spiritual in human affairs, and have let it be obscured by emphasis on the physical and material. An especially vivid imagination is needed to appreciate the truth that human goods are more effectively obtained by co-operation than by conflict.

But as men develop an understanding of their own spiritual nature, the importance of the common interest and of the distant future is more easily appreciated. The habit of thinking in terms of spiritual goods, frees us from subservience to the present and to the proximate. The training of men's minds and spirits cannot be effected overnight. The advancement of human knowledge is a matter requiring long planning. It is no accident that of all aspects of human life, those least limited by group, national, or institutional considerations are involved in the pursuit of truth, in the arts, and in religious thinking.

The history of civilization may be viewed as an effort by man to free himself from bondage to material concerns. Primitive man regards the immortal element in himself as a "shade" or "ghost," a form of being resembling his material body, but not quite as real. He regards the intangibility of his spirit as a deficiency, which more than offsets its immortality. Men took many generations to conclude that, if man has a spirit, it must be far more important than the body; because the spirit and not the body gives man meaning. Yet even today after twenty centuries of emphasis on the spiritual nature of man and the immortality of his soul, the use of the term, "ghost," for the spirit of the dead reminds us of the primitive tendency to regard the body as in some way superior to the spirit.

Our difficulty in appreciating the nature of the human spirit is of a piece with that which confronts us in thinking of the whole realm of the spiritual world. It is comparatively easy to make men aware of human suffering from famine; but it is difficult to make them as keenly aware of the widespread suffering caused by lack of knowledge. We may be able to persuade our fellow countrymen of the urgent importance of feeding the starving of Europe and Asia, and of denying ourselves some food to save lives. But it seems more difficult to persuade ourselves that both we and the rest of the world are facing disaster for failure to meet the challenging need of our time for better men. Many proposals are now being made to train men to increase our war potential in terms of industrial and scientific research. It is difficult to find any suggestion that men should be trained to increase our peace potential in terms of more

capable and more understanding peacemakers, educators, philoso
phers, and human beings. But the urgent need of the hour is not so
much a superatomic bomb or a faster plane as men able to guide
mankind from the morass where the solution to all problems must
lie in self-destruction.

The one way to make men spiritually minded is for some of us to
attain to that state ourselves. If we can persuade ourselves not only
intellectually, but also emotionally, that the human spirit and spiritual
values are the truly important aspects of life, we will find others to
follow that concept. We will be able to make our fellow citizens, and
our fellow men of other nations, realize that interest in material things
divides mankind, while interest in spiritual things unites them. This
is natural, for of material things there is a limited supply to meet an
unlimited need, while to spiritual things there can be no limit, for
we create them ourselves. There is an infinite amount of knowledge
to be attained; there is an infinite number of good deeds to be per-
formed; man has infinite potentialities for creation in esthetics and
literature. When men seem to be divided because of spiritual issues,
we may be sure that the real source of division is the hunger for
power or prestige, and that the issues of the spiritual life are being
used to conceal an urge for unspiritual ends. The wars of religion
themselves were fought for unreligious ends; men are not divided
but united by the goals of serving God.

The problem of building a secure civilization thus resolves itself into a consideration of three neglected aspects of human life in
our day. We must reorient ourselves to think of the good of the
whole as not only more important than the good of the part, but as
in itself the only real good the part can enjoy. We must discover how
men may become as passionate about future goods as they are about
these of immediate concern. We must train ourselves to be more
concerned about the spiritual welfare of man, than about his physical
welfare; for, if man's spiritual problems are solved, the physical ones
will be solved. But if man concentrates on material problems, he
will endanger his material existence and lose his spiritual life.

Civilization for the future may well depend on the extent to which
we can free ourselves from concern with the matters which appear

to be most urgent—the problems of today, the problems of our special groups, and the problems of the material world—so that we may give ourselves to the fundamental matters now overlooked—the problems of tomorrow, the problems of the whole race, and the problems of the spiritual life.

II

THE RISE OF AN AMERICAN CULTURE

BY

ALLAN NEVINS

In his massive work *A Study of History,* Arnold Toynbee, with a wealth of illustrations drawn from the past, gives us his interpretation both of the main factors in the origin and rise of civilization and of the principal causes of the progressive decline and final death of many national cultures. It will be remembered that he finds all great civilizations of the past dependent upon what he calls the law of "Challenge and Response"; the law, that is, that no people can rise to greatness unless it is stimulated to activity by peril, by harshness of environment, by political, economic, or geographic difficulties. He traces the flowering of a civilization, in broad terms, to the success of a creative minority of leaders in firing the majority with its own dynamic energy, its inspiring vision. When a nation is too prosperous, when the conditions of its life are too easy, when it is not constantly compelled to grapple with new difficulties, it is certain to become softer in fibre, to lose the power to rise higher and higher, and to show a diminishing faith in its own future. If its creative minority ceases to be alert and ambitious leaders become merely a privileged class, a "dominant minority," then they lose influence over the majority, disunity sets in, and decay begins. Such, in sweeping outlines, is Dr. Toynbee's analysis of the main elements in the rise and decline of national civilizations.

The rise of a national civilization is one problem; the formation of a national character is another. That nations of a roughly equivalent civilization do have distinctly different characters, and that national character has something to do with the durability of a civilization, there can be no doubt. We need only look at the world about us, in what Winston Churchill calls "all its wonder and all its woe." The national character of Germany today, darkened and debased by National Socialism and by certain other sinister influences which can be traced at least as far back as Bismarck, has exhibited certain well-defined traits. We need not consider the German character irreclaimable; but it assuredly took on some terrible lineaments. The national character of France in 1940 just as clearly showed some elements of decadence. Ernest Renan had said in 1888, looking at some of the unhappiest tendencies of that day: "France is dying, do not trouble her agony." She was not dying, and we all expect to see her resurgence; but her recent calamities did spring from evident flaws of character. The national character of Russia has impressed the world, and so has that of Great Britain. Both the Russian and British peoples rose to the demands of an unexampled crisis with a fortitude, a devotion, a stubbornness, and a dashing gallantry that have written some of the finest pages in history. We knew of old— we have known for generations past—that we could depend upon the British character, but we have discovered in the Russian character certain treasures that we were hardly certain existed.

The determinates of national character are of course varied and complex. History, tradition, religious faith, economic circumstances, geography, and climate all play a part; so do political and social institutions. A great body of determinates unites to form what we call a system, and this system is more powerful than any individuals in it. Hence it is that we should watch carefully the kind of tradition, the kind of institution, that we allow to grow up to help form the national character. John Fiske once enunciated a striking maxim. "While it is true," he wrote, "though many people do not know it, that by no imaginable artifice can you make a society that is better than the human units you put into it, it is also true that nothing is easier than to make a society that is worse than its units." The individual German is in millions of instances just as good a man as the individual Swede, or the individual Swiss; but Sweden and Switzerland have systems or societies that make for a healthy, wholesome civilization, while Germany has had a system that makes for an evil society. Just so, in ancient times, the individual Spartan was no doubt often just as good a man as the individual Athenian; but Sparta had a system which produced a repellent national character, while the Athenian system flowered into unsurpassed beauties and graces.

One of the clearest contrasts between two different types of national character is that drawn by Francis Parkman between the civilization of the old régime in French Canada and the civilization of the British colonies on the eastern seaboard of the present United States. The French system in old Canada was one of rigid bureaucratic tyranny, touching and warping every form of human activity. It was summed up in Louis XIV's boast, "The state is myself." The government, and a highly centralized government at that, controlled everything—agriculture, industry, business, the schools, the church, the very amount of the bride's dowry and the size of the citizen's house and the quantity of his furniture. No room was left for individual initiative, for local self-control, for the automatic and natural expansion of communities into states and states into nations. The system was narrow, aggressive, rigidly planned, and despotic. The system in the British colonies of North America, on the other hand, was loose, unshackled, individualistic, and pre-eminently industrial. The fullest scope was given to initiative and resourcefulness. Communities were allowed to govern themselves and taught to value freedom. They developed a resilience and energy unknown in French Canada. The individual leaders of French America were quite as courageous, as patriotic, as farsighted, and as bold, as the individual leaders of the thirteen colonies. Men like Cadillac, Bienville, Iberville, Laval, Montcalm, possessed virtues of an heroic cast. But the system that dominated French Canada produced a national character, or rather a colonial character, markedly inferior to the system that dominated British America; and when the two grappled in a dramatic series of wars, the former was overwhelmed.

Very frequently the distinction between two different national characters is much less strongly marked. It was recently my fortune to spend six months in Australia and New Zealand. Any visitor to those two remarkable countries, so vigorous, progressive, and hopeful, must be struck by the fact that they are so like the United States, and at the same time so unlike. Outwardly, the American and Australasian peoples possess much the same principles, tastes, and aims. They have many characteristics in common. Both are intensely democratic and egalitarian, deeming all men equal and detesting all class lines. Indeed, the Australians and New Zealanders are even more aggressively democratic than most Americans. Both they and we have the same strong regard for representative self-government. They talk of the weaknesses of Parliament as we talk of the weaknesses of Congress, but neither they nor we would think of abolishing these "talking shops." The Australasians and the Americans have the same powerful devotion to civil liberties. There, as here, the rights of freedom of speech, freedom of the press, freedom of worship, and free assemblage are taken for granted and, when assailed, are fiercely defended. But there is one cardinal difference between the national character of Americans and that of Australians and New Zealanders. For several clear and natural reasons, they take a very different and more "advanced" attitude toward the role of the state in social and economic affairs. They expect and welcome a larger amount of government intervention in the industrial sphere, a more vigorous provision by the state for basic human welfare. The whole climate of opinion on these matters is different from that which exists in America. From the beginning, in the Antipodes, the state played a larger part, both in promoting settlement and in protecting settlers, than it did in the United States. The result is that the national character of Australia and New Zealand differs very clearly, though not very radically, from that of the United States.

What is the national character of Americans, and what, if any, are the changes it has undergone in the series of crises which have overtaken the republic since 1914? These are difficult questions. Several men, including Frank E. Hill and James Truslow Adams, have now published books intended to answer the query, "What is American?" They have not fared too successfully with their responses. Our language is borrowed from Britain. Our literature, down at least to recent times, bears the strong imprint of British influences and origins. Our political institutions and laws, while in part indigenous, are in still larger part of British type and flavor.

Our general culture is full of borrowings, as in music from Germany, in art from Italy and France, in education from a half-dozen countries. In most respects our civilization seems but a branch of the great main stem of European civilization. Nevertheless, we are quite warranted in asserting that we do have a national spirit or character that is essentially American. It is not difficult to describe, but the best way to define it is by pointing to its sources—for its sources make clear its general nature. Americans always believe in the unique quality of their civilization, and they trace it to certain unique factors.

One of the principle factors, of course, has been their frontier experience. The molding power of the frontier upon American character has been most fully pointed out by Frederick J. Turner, although the idea can be traced back to older writers—to James Bryce, to Edwin L. Godkin, and even to the philosopher Hegel, writing in the 1820's. Before Turner, historians were concerned chiefly with what the pioneer did to the frontier—with the way in which he pushed back the bounds of savagery and conquered the wilderness. Turner showed that the more significant matter was what the frontier did to the settler; that, while in one sense the pioneer conquered the wilderness, in another sense the wilderness conquered and changed the pioneer. He demonstrated that a whole series of American generations, from 1620 to 1890, passed through a whole series of frontiers, from the seaboard frontier of the Pilgrims and Puritans to the Great Plains frontier of the ranchers. And what did the frontier do to these rolling waves of American humanity? It was a huge and active mixing-bowl of races, wherein many stocks—British, Irish, German, Scandinavian, French Huguenot—commingled their blood. It was a great school of egalitarian democracy, every man being precisely as good as his neighbor. It was a potent teacher of nationalism and patriotism, for on the frontier men regarded themselves not as New Yorkers, Georgians, or Ohioans, but as Americans. It taught men to be individualistic, self-reliant, practical, and resourceful.

The frontier affected the American character not only by passing successive generations through a great school of racial tolerance, egalitarian democracy, nationalism, and individual initiative; it also affected the American character by its indirect impress on the industrial society of the East. Emigration to the frontier kept wages higher and conditions of work better than they would otherwise have been. Any mechanic who grew discontented with his treatment or who suffered from seasonal unemployment could preëmpt a farm in the newer regions. "The West," wrote a Philadelphia observer in 1857, "is full of examples of what has been done and is being done by poor men, mechanics, and particularly young men." Much has been written upon the safety-valve theory of frontier emigration. It is highly doubtful that any considerable body of Eastern wage earners ever removed to Western farms. But it is certain that the empty West did drain off a great deal of labor that but for the free lands would have gone into industrial pursuits. It is also undoubtedly true that the existence of the empty West as a field into which unhappy wage earners could escape, had a psychological effect upon these workers, making them more independent and self-assertive. In short, the frontier, so long as it lasted, prevented the American worker from being proletarianized—from being held down to the unhappy level of the wage earners in continental Europe. It made possible better wage-scales, higher standards of living, and a more hopeful outlook; and in this indirect fashion, too, it helped mold the American character.

The nature of American immigration also shaped our national character, and this for two reasons. To begin with, immigration for a good many generations probably sifted out the hardier and more ambitious Europeans for the American stock. It is true that some students believe that after the first strong settlements were made this was hardly true; that many came to America because they failed to make a success of life in the Old World, because they were weak, indolent, and maladjusted. But the weight of evidence seems to point to a special energy and independence among the immigrant stocks. Down to 1850 at least, it required distinct initiative and hardiness to cross the ocean. The rebellious-spirited man was more likely to migrate than the docile, easy-going citizen. And, in the second place, this migration was a migration of individuals, not of communities. Men and women came singly, not, as to New Zealand, by whole townships. They had to learn from the outset to fend for themselves, and most of them delighted to do so. Instead of looking to community provision for their safety and comfort, they looked to their own strong right arms.

A third factor in giving the American character its special traits was freedom of enterprise. Newcomers to America found a land unburdened by any traces of the feudal economy. Lands were never held in common, after the old European system; at least, they were almost never so held after the settlers at Jamestown and Plymouth found that communal ownership was a failure. We had a manorial land system in the Hudson Valley and in parts of the South, but in general American agriculture was patterned on the small freehold farm, tilled with complete freedom of enterprise. The same freedom existed for industrial workers and artisans. In the seventeenth and even in the first half of the eighteenth century, craft gilds, controlling apprenticeship, wages, and conditions of labor, were powerful in England. On the continent of Europe they maintained their grip much later. But in the American colonies men could readily embark on any craft or trade they pleased to take up, and could pursue it in their own ways. Mediaeval restraints were little known, and, though in time monopolies grew up, they never had, as in Europe, the sanction of the state.

This freedom of enterprise created another school of individualism —an industrial school, matching that of the frontier. It was through this school that millions of latter-day immigrants passed. They were apprenticed to mill, forge, and factory as the earlier immigrants had been apprenticed to wilderness and prairie. Some obvious resemblances exist between Andrew Jackson, son of the Tennessee frontier, and Alfred E. Smith, son of the New York fish market. The later immigrants found life as rough and hard as did the Scotch-Irish hunters in buckskin leggings. They found peril, for more men have been killed by the machine than were ever killed by the red Indians. Those who relied on qualities other than aggressive individualism were impatiently left behind; the path to safety was the path of self-assertion and hard hitting.

The older and the newer stocks of the United States hold very different images of the country and its history; but these images are alike in emphasizing freedom of enterprise. Looking back, the older stock sees a succession of grim fighters like Miles Standish, or Robert Rogers, or Daniel Boone, or Kit Carson. This older stock pictures its ancestors as plunging from the seaboard into the dense forest that Cooper painted; hewing out wilderness roads, and launching steamboats on the rivers; battling with panthers and savages; crossing the prairies and arid plains; outfacing the blizzard and slaying the buffalo. In the wake of the pioneer his sons and daughters built up the farms he had cleared and the towns he had founded, carrying on his tradition of energetic individualism. The America of these pioneers was a land of green forests, grassy plains, and clear air. It was an America full of rude plenty: shelter for the felling of the trees, food for the tillage, and land for the mere taking. The hardships bred endurance and toughness, but they gave way in a generation to comfort and security.

The children of the later immigration see a pioneer, too. But he was a man with a pick, a puddling rod, or a monkey wrench. He found his way not to shady forest or waving prairie, but to a mill village set amid smoke, cinders, and weeds, a slumlike street where he breathed foul air and touched grime. He had to fight against all the exploitations that Jurgen met in Upton Sinclair's *The Jungle*. His environment was far less plastic than that of the forest pioneer. But the newcomers of this later stock, like the first comers, developed an intense and stubborn individualism. It was merely a different type of individualism. There had been an easy, hopeful, good-tempered quality inherent in the individualism of the Western frontiersman, a quality pictured in the breezy and often rollicking stories that Edward Eggleston, Mark Twain, and Bret Harte wrote about him. But the individualist of the later stock, whether labor leader, socialist agitator, small businessman, or simply workman, had a less expansive and optimistic quality. His moods were tinged with gloom, and he regarded the world with a certain admixture of suspicion and irony. It was the irony that Carl Sandburg captured when he wrote that industrialized Chicago, toolmaker and stacker of wheat, "fished from its depths a text: 'Independent as a hog on ice.' "

The tradition of free enterprise reached its apogee in the fierce release of industrial energy that occurred between the Civil War and the First World War. The industrial revolution overswept the United States with tremendous force and transformed it with astonishing speed from a predominantly agricultural nation to an overwhelmingly business nation. That revolution was but well started when the Civil War began, and the war pushed it forward with headlong impetus. The steel industry, the petroleum industry, the wheat-milling and meat-packing industries, sprang up like giants. Railroads were built from side to side of the continent, great cities were created, factories were expanded, invention was accelerated, all on such a scale as the world had never before seen. In one generation the region west of the Missouri was transformed from a waste into a rich mineral and agricultural empire. Individual initiative, though often shockingly lawless, served the country well during this period. It changed the whole face of the continent, created wealth in unprecedented bulk, and made the United States the strongest industrial nation on the globe. The individualistic businessman acquired enormous power. In the days of McKinley and Hanna he seemed to be taking control even of the national government. It was easy for free enterprise, for economic individualism, to become more aggressive and unrestrained in America than anywhere else in the world. In Britain, Germany, and other old lands a great landed aristocracy had the support of the squirearchy and the junkers in holding their own against industry and business. The United States had no such groups, and the free enterpriser swept everything before him.

Another element—a complementary element—in shaping the American national character was the tradition of a noninterfering state. The seventeenth and eighteenth-century settlers who came to America from Europe left behind them lands which were dominated by mercantilist theory. Most of them were outspoken rebels against mercantilism. So long as the thirteen colonies were part of the British Empire, mercantilism in the broad view could be supported by a number of imposing arguments. It had real meaning. But it implied that the well-being of the state was more important than the well-being of the individual and that the state should constantly interfere with the activities of the individual. Allegiance to mercantilism was never strong in the American colonies. It grew weaker till in the latter part of the eighteenth century many colonists were in open revolt against it. The American Revolution struck down mercantilism completely in America in the same year, 1776, that Adam Smith by the publication of his *Wealth of Nations* dealt it a mortal blow in Great Britain. The Revolution was not merely a political revolt against an interfering state; it was an economic revolt against an interfering state. Emerging from that revolution, the former colonists naturally regarded the strong state with suspicion and took steps to guard themselves against it. The first state constitutions set up governments of a noninterfering type, governments which would leave the decent, law-abiding individual alone. The Federal Constitution, by irresistible popular demand, was given a Bill of Rights. The forces long dominant in the political life of the young republic—the forces led by Thomas Jefferson and Andrew Jackson—supported the idea of the weak or noninterfering state.

It was not until the 1840's, when the Corn Laws were repealed, that Adam Smith's ideas completely conquered the mercantilist principle in Great Britain. The principle of the absolute state remained powerful in France until after the downfall of Napoleon III. The principle of authoritarian state power was never really overthrown in Germany. But in the United States the tradition of free enterprise never had to adjust itself, as it did in Australia and New Zealand, to an equally strong tradition of state interference. From 1776 right down to 1900 and after, the state remained weak in relation to all the economic rights and privileges of the individual. Efforts to strengthen state power in the Granger Laws of the 1870's, in the Interstate Commerce Act of 1887, and in the Sherman Anti-Trust Act of 1890 were ineffectual; the weak state continued to be an element in the formation of national character until this century.

Still other elements which contributed to the molding of the American character might be mentioned. One was the ideal of equality; not in the sense of equality of talents, or fortune, but of a rough equality of opportunity. In theory, and to a great extent in practice, we have always kept the ladder clear for aspiring merit to climb. One of the principal impulses behind the establishment of free public education in the United States was the desire to protect equality of opportunity; to give the poor boy as good a chance as the rich. Till near the end of the nineteenth century, the existence of a great area of free or nearly free public lands, uncontrolled by any landlord, meant a definite contribution to equality of opportunity. Down to our own time, the possibility of starting in business with little capital or none, as Carnegie, Rockefeller, Harriman, Hill, Henry Ford, Henry Kaiser all started, did much to guarantee equality of opportunity.

And in one sense the grandest of all the factors shaping the national character has been the ingrained belief of Americans in fundamental civil rights, a belief inherited largely from the British forbears of the early settlers. The circumstances under which the British Colonies were founded made for a generous degree of racial, religious, and political toleration. Rhode Island as established by Roger Williams and Pennsylvania by William Penn were asylums in which men of all Protestant faiths held an equal freedom. Maryland was established as a colony in which Catholics should hold the same rights as Protestants. Charleston, New York, and Newport were early centers of the Jewish faith. People from every country of Europe were welcomed in the colonies on a general plane of equality. Freedom of speech, assemblage, and petition were generally respected. Rights of minorities were fairly well safeguarded, if only by traditions of compromise. When the United States set up its own government, the first ten amendments to the Constitution guaranteed the fullest civil and religious privileges. Americans have therefore always felt a stern repugnance for intolerance in any form. We need only think how much our fierce belief in civil freedom and toleration did to place the United States in a position of hostility to Nazi Germany, in order to realize how deeply this belief has affected our national character.

It is by some such analysis as this that we can really establish the special traits of American character and answer the question whether in recent times it has changed. It does not do to fasten our attention upon mere superficial characteristics or the traits of notable individuals or groups. George Bernard Shaw satirized the ordinary glib generalizations about the gaiety of the French, the stolidity of the Germans, the gloominess of the Russians, in his introduction to "John Bull's Other Island." The Irish, he wrote, were regarded as emotional and outspoken; the British as serious and taciturn. Yet it was the Irish Wellington who never uttered a jest nor betrayed a feeling, while it was the English Nelson who acted and spoke impetuously, loved with gay abandon, and died saying, "Kiss me, Hardy." We need not attach much importance to the list of outward American traits compiled by every foreign observer in America. This list includes the energy, tension, and strenuosity which led the Frenchman de Tocqueville more than a century ago to speak of the "strange unrest" of Americans, and the German Hugo Munsterberg to trace even the habits of gum-chewing and using rocking chairs to "motor restlessness." It includes such alleged characteristics as Puritanism, braggadocio, and addiction to violence—characteristics which, if they exist, do not run deep. What really count are those elements of character traceable to the deep forces above enumerated. They are the traits of individualism, enterprise, belief in equality of opportunity, devotion to personal freedom in all that pertains to civil and religious rights, and optimism—the optimism born of a sense that horizons are wider in America than elsewhere, that life is freer, and that chances to rise are more abundant.

If, of all these traits, we fix our eyes upon two, the unrestrained individualism and the warm, ebullient optimism which were undoubtedly long prominent in America, we can begin to answer the question whether the national character has undergone any recent changes. These two elements of the American character have always operated together. The optimism has bulwarked the individualism, and the individualism has strengthened the optimism. It is clear to any student of American history that their collaboration has been exceedingly effective—that it accomplished wonders in the years when we were making the most of our great national resources and developing the country. They were largely responsible for the speed and energy with which we built up our civilization. When President Hoover's Committee on Recent Economic Changes published its book on that subject in 1929, its members undertook to point out what educated Europeans envied in the American system. They emphasized this dominant national trait of optimistic energy, writing: "The individual in America is mobile as to place and calling; he is moving upward. . . . The way to education and to promotion is wide open; indeed, many ladders to advancement are available, and their rungs are all intact, so that he may climb who will." But even as the committee was so writing, men were coming to doubt whether the collaboration would continue to be effective—whether, in especial, the unrestrained individualism ought not to be placed under clear state restraints. What future historians may well call the Period of Recurrent Crisis—the period of the First World War, the Great Boom, the Great Depression, and the Second World War—was producing a new attitude.

For by the time of the First World War the nation had become crowded—as crowded as much of the Old World. The disappearance of free land had long since ended the opportunities of the frontier. The natural resources, once squandered so carelessly, no longer seemed illimitable. In the modern economy of the United States such phrases as "free enterprise" and "equality of opportunity," often took on a hollow, ironic ring. Because of the nation's wide array of marginal industries and luxury industries, not millions but tens of millions were at the mercy of economic fluctuations. The events of the years just after 1914, and still more of those just after 1929, proved that if the nation failed to provide in time against abrupt strains and terrible stresses, it might suffer the heaviest disaster. And how could it so provide except by state action that would sharply limit the old individualism? To guard against calamity, careful planning in advance and social co-operation on the largest scale were imperative necessities. Just as Washington's generation had to face an outlook very different from that existing before the Declaration of Independence, and Lincoln's generation an outlook very different from that existing before the Emancipation Proclamation, so the Period of the Recurrent Crisis confronted Americans with a wholly new set of conditions and tasks. Did they need changes in the national character to meet them? Even as this question was being asked, it was being unmistakably answered; at least one great change was occurring.

The new tests and tasks and the need for a responsive change had been foreseen a generation earlier by James Bryce. In writing the last pages of his *American Commonwealth,* Bryce had ventured a prediction. It was expressed in a metaphor. The westward-faring traveler from Europe to America, he remarked, traverses a thousand miles of clear sea under open skies. But at a certain point in the voyage, looking ahead, he sees a dim dark line upon the face of the ocean. It is the line of cloud and fog hanging over the Grand Banks. Soon the vessel leaves the bright sunlight and plunges into the clammy embrace of this gloomy belt, concealing treacherous shallows and dangerous icebergs. Just so, predicted Bryce, the American republic, after a long voyage on sunny seas, would shortly plunge into a belt of gloom and trial. During its first century the nation had been blessed with huge areas of untaken fertile land and mineral wealth, a rich heritage for a still uncrowded population. But the time was at hand when the land and the mines would all be taken; when population would become dense; when immense industrial agglomerations, suffering from want and discontent, would be as important a feature of American as of European life. When we entered this Shadow Belt, wrote Bryce, the true test of our institutions would come, which every observer must await with anxiety. It was a test, he implied, which might well call for modifications of the national character. He was right. We were on the fringe of the Shadow Belt in 1900, we were fairly in its embrace by 1914, and we found ourselves much deeper still when the Great Depression of 1930 smote us.

It was in response to an exigent set of needs that the great series of governmental innovations which we call the New Deal was introduced; a series that really began under Herbert Hoover, but was carried much further by Franklin D. Roosevelt. In its way, this series of innovations was almost revolutionary. The whole concept of the relation between the state (that is, the national government) and society at large was profoundly altered. "The state had previously been a negative or impartial force, seeking to stand aloof from the contests in the market place, or at best offering only its mediation to see that principles of equity and justice were preserved, and it had refused to interfere in the interests of the security and welfare of its laboring peoples. Now it became the interventionist state. It imposed on the free business enterpriser all sorts of controls and regulations; it entered freely into business itself, often as competitor with private corporations; it used its great fiscal and financial powers to redistribute wealth and to create income; it committed itself to an elaborate program of social security that offered protection, in time, to the whole population against the mischances of unemployment, invalidism, and sudden death, and from the cradle to the grave. The *laissez-faire* state with only a skeletal apparatus of offices and agencies had become the social-service state with a vast and intricately contrived and permanent machinery of officers and bureaucrats." Why? Not merely because of the sudden emergency of 1930 and the succeeding years, terrible as that was, but because Americans had been realizing ever since 1900 that they were indeed in the Shadow Belt, facing the problems that older and more crowded populations had faced before them; because the American character, under the pressure of the new conditions, had been changing.

The great central innovation of the new period ought to be clearly identified. It did not lie in Mr. Roosevelt's measures for the regulation of business by the government. Such measures can be traced back to Woodrow Wilson, Theodore Roosevelt, and even to earlier presidents. It did not lie in the new measures of relief and rehabilitation undertaken by the government; precedents for them could also be found in the past. Nor did it lie in Mr. Roosevelt's patent sympathy with the underprivileged, and his desire to restore governmental power to the democratic masses. In this sympathy and this desire he was merely carrying on the traditions of Lincoln, Andrew Jackson, and Thomas Jefferson. It lay rather in the new conception of the state as a powerful equilibrizing agent, a force which must intervene to help private enterprise save itself from disaster. This was the heart of the new conception of the interventionist state. Once the great mass of Americans accepted the principle that recovery was no longer automatic, that the state must intervene to restore prosperity, they also (as Mr. Walter Lippmann has pointed out) accepted the principle that the state has a right to intervene to maintain prosperity; that is, the state must concern itself constantly with the economy of the nation, helping to plan and to control it. This new principle was not introduced by Mr. Roosevelt; it was rather sponsored and recommended by Mr. Hoover when he and Congress acted to create the Reconstruction Finance Corporation. From that moment the United States was committed to something which it had previously avoided —to the interventionist state.

All this pointed to a change in the national character. The old devotion to individual enterprise, unaided and unhampered, as the specific for all ills, was gone. The American people had come to realize that thereafter their civilization would have to be less individualistic and would have to cultivate a more social and co-operative spirit. They had begun to realize this in the days of Theodore Roosevelt, who was a great preacher of social justice, and who used the state to maintain justice. They had harkened to a long list of social reformers —Golden Rule Jones, Tom Johnson, Jacob Riis, Lincoln Steffens, John Spargo, Brand Whitlock, Samuel Gompers, Eugene V. Debs— who were apostles not of individualism, but of the social virtues. They had watched the bold experiments made in kindred lands; in New Zealand under King Dick Seddon, in Great Britain under David Lloyd George. Their thinking had been modified by the mass immigration which came from the crowded lands of eastern and southern Europe after the closing of our frontier. They had become accustomed in the First World War to the idea that the state might take the whole national life under its control to meet a great crisis. The war could not have been fought to early victory without a tremendous regimentation of effort: without the War Industries Board, the War Labor Board, the food and fuel controls, the government management of railroads, and all the rest. When the conflict ended, the nation tried to escape back to "normalcy"—but the memory of its wartime experience lingered.

How much the national character had altered, and how totally dead was the old ideal of unrestrained individualism, became evident when the presidential campaign of 1940 was fought out. For in that campaign the Republican Party, while fiercely criticizing the *methods* which the Democratic Administration had used in carrying out its policies, tacitly accepted the main *ideas* below those policies. The change was one of the most momentous in our history. Nor was it a change for the worse. Debate would of course rage, as it is still raging, over the exact limits to be set to the action of the state. But the new social and co-operative ideals were here to stay. The now crowded nation, turning its back on its happy adolescence, was squarely facing the grim problems of its maturity.

III

WHAT COMMON GROUND HAS AMERICA WON?

BY

LAWRENCE K. FRANK

This is indeed a difficult theme because any assertion of a common ground that has been won will almost surely be challenged by references to the many conflicts and rivalries, the animosities and hatreds, and the persistence of minority groups. Indeed, the next four lectures in this series on "Threats to American Unity" show how difficult it is to speak of any common ground.

Perhaps it would be more appropriate to ask what common ground are we *winning* as a basis for American unity.

The major theme of this series is "Unity and Difference in American Life." Now the democratic faith cherishes a belief in the dignity and worth of the individual and, therefore, must not only recognize but encourage individual differences and diversities of all kinds. But, if we hope to maintain social order, we must find or create some unity, at least in the form of some basic assumptions, some common values, some generally accepted patterns of human relationships that are compatible with the dignity and worth of the individual.

Here it may be appropriate to point out that social order is not a superhuman cosmic organization existing somewhere between the earth and sky and operating through large-scale social forces. Those are just figures of speech, metaphors derived from an earlier day which, unfortunately, we too often interpret literally.

Social order is in people, in us, and it exists in accordance with what people believe and do and do not do, the way they feel and how they aspire. So long as we think of social order as external, as something outside of people, we tend to think of how individuals must be fitted

into or made to adjust to the existing scheme of things as expressed
in our social, economic, and political organizations and practices.
We are also apt to think of social order as demanding a high degree
of uniformity of belief, action, and speech, and we tend to emphasize
the need of coercing individuals into conformity. Now it is true that
some kinds of social order are maintained by regimentation, by an
enforced conformity to prescribed patterns and suppression of any
deviations therefrom. Indeed, as will be pointed out later, that has
been the predominant pattern of social order in the past, and today
some among us still incline to that kind of social order that is based
on rigid uniformity. It is not difficult to find individuals or groups
who want everyone else to believe, to think, to act, and to feel, according to a prescribed model which they prefer and which they wish
to impose upon all others. The democratic approach to social order,
on the other hand, is essentially that of achieving order by or-
chestrating the widest diversities of individuality on the common
theme of human needs and values. Thus, we may think of social
order not as something already given and established, a part of nature,
but as that which must be achieved and maintained by all members
of the group in their conduct and, especially, in all their interpersonal
relationships.

Since these first three lectures are retrospective, it will be appropriate to look back at our past history as representatives of Western
European cultural traditions and at the past and, to a certain extent,
the present, of other cultural groups. When we do look back we see
that all over the world different societies have been established upon
the basis of a rigid hierarchy of rank, caste, class, and privilege,
according to the fixed status of each individual. Social orders, in
other words, have been developed and maintained in terms of super-
ordination and subordination, of dominance and submission. A few
privileged individuals have exercised power and control over the
many who have been kept in a condition of slavery and serfdom or
of inferior subordinate positions. In such societies those at the top
have exercised control over those beneath them who, in turn, submit
to such dominance and exploitation as their lot in life in this kind
of social order, because these relationships are not only sanctioned

by law and government and by custom but also by their religion.

Except for a few of the smaller cultures, this has been the pattern of social order throughout the world. Not only in other cultures but in our own Western European culture, social order has been based upon a fixed status in which the king and the nobles or the government have ruled over the lives of the majority of people. We need only remember the doctrine of the divine right of kings and how the individual who belonged to the lower orders was taught to obey, to be submissive, to accept whatever those on top decreed, often with religious sanction.

It was not until the seventeenth and eighteenth centuries that the concept of individual rights and of personal freedom really emerged to become the basis for the ensuing struggle for individual liberty. We need only recall how slow has been the extension of the franchise, how slowly and reluctantly we have achieved religious freedom, how many of the older disabilities and limitations and discriminations still survive.

Here let me call to your attention the two largest "minority" groups in our society today, groups which for generations have been deprived of the rights which we now recognize as essential to human dignity, long subject to domination, exploitation, and often humiliation, with little or no personal freedom or enjoyment of personal integrity. I refer, of course, to women and children. Let me remind you that only recently have women gained such elementary legal rights as the power to contract, to own property, to control their own income, to vote, to have access to college and professional education, to participate in public affairs, to choose their own husbands, and to decide what they wished to do with their own lives. Let us remember all the opposition and the arguments and the sanctions that were invoked to oppose every one of these steps in their emancipation.

While women have begun to emerge from their former status as a minority group, children are still subject to all the disabilities and disadvantages of a minority group. They are still subject to whatever their parents may wish to do to them; and as the child-guidance clinics and the juvenile courts and the social agencies will testify, children today are exposed to almost incredible brutality, humiliation, degradation, and other forms of distortion. We are still very far from recognizing the dignity and worth of the personality of children, of according them the respect as personalities which is essential to a free society.

It must never be forgotten that in this older hierarchal society of fixed status, of a few dominating the many, no one felt guilty. It was the right and the duty of the superior, sanctioned by law and the church, and demanded by loyalty to his class, to exercise such control over others, to see that people were kept in their places. Likewise, those who were dominated and exploited often felt unhappy and bitter but they accepted their lot with little or no feeling of being humiliated, of being treated unjustly, because that treatment was what they were taught to expect.

It is worth remembering that except for occasional revolts, those who were most heavily burdened and most inhumanly treated, rarely protested against what was happening to them.

Today as we look back we see how the older society of fixed status has been gradually breaking down over the past two or three centuries. The privileges, the authority, the vested right and power, have been crumbling. The older conception of divine right of kings and of nobles, the older feudal society, the older legal control by the few exercising unlimited power, have been going. Indeed, we must stop and remember that not very long ago the old master-servant relationship was the dominant one in all fields of employment, with apprentices bound by indentures, subject to the master's rule and discipline. Even today we have peonage, not far removed from the older slavery which has, at least officially, been abolished.

What is of major significance in this context is that formerly the conduct of all interpersonal relationships was patterned and guided by fixed rules of conduct according to the status of the individuals involved. There was a well-established code in which individuals were always treated according to their membership in a particular class or caste or group, and those who occupied the inferior position were expected to conform, to submit, to acquiesce, in being used, misused, dominated, and exploited by those who occupied the superior position.

With the passing of this older fixed status and the increasing repudiation of the sanctions that once sustained that kind of society, we are faced with confusion, with conflicts, with insecurity and anxiety in every area of life.

For the first time we are being faced with an exigent situation, confronted with the relatively new problem of how we are to conduct our interpersonal relationships with others *as persons,* as individuals. Today we are struggling to establish patterns of human relationships to replace the older stereotyped patterns based upon fixed status and group membership.

Thus, we may say that today no one really knows what and how to act because there are no clear, well-defined patterns for his or her guidance, and we have had little or no practice in acting toward others, *as personalities.* Thus, in so many areas we must weigh, evaluate, and reflect and deliberately decide how to act and speak and conduct our affairs with other personalities. We must develop a new awareness and new sensibilities so that we will realize how others feel and will understand that they, too, have aspirations.

Thus we see what I like to call the two insecurities. There is the insecurity and confusion of the formerly dominant or majority groups who politically, economically, and socially are uncertain what to do and how to act. They are uncertain and often resentful because they still cling to many of the older traditions and they are disturbed because others do not accept their prestige and their supposed superiority. Moreover, there is much insecurity and often acute anxiety felt by individuals who cannot tolerate having other people believe and think and act in patterns different from their own. Their anxiety becomes so great that at times they wish to compel others to accept their beliefs and to follow their patterns. Sometimes in their endeavor to accommodate to changing circumstances they become patronizing and when rebuffed they become hard-boiled and cynical. I venture to suggest there is a great deal of insecurity among the so-called majority groups in our society today.

The formerly submissive, exploited minorities are also insecure because they are uncertain how to act. They are not sure they are really accepted or that they belong, so that they fluctuate between the older deferential conduct and the new patterns, and sometimes become openly truculent with a "chip on the shoulder," as so many have observed. They also are insecure and uncertain how far they can go, worried lest they be rebuffed and yet anxious not to slip back into their former position of inferiority.

These are the two polarized positions of insecurity, but all of us are confused and uncertain because we have not yet developed the patterns of human relationship that accord with our democratic aspirations.

Thus, we may say our minority problems, our tensions between groups, are symptoms of a changing social order in which we are striving to develop a new basis of human relationships. Here we should recognize what is of very great significance, namely, that those who have been dominated and exploited, who have been subordinated, do not feel humiliated or degraded, do not consider themselves unfairly and unjustly treated, until they begin to develop a sense of their own worth and dignity and a feeling that they are personalities. This is significant because it means that people of all groups who were formerly oppressed and disadvantaged are now gaining a sense of their own value and place in life, are developing respect of themselves as personalities, to which our democratic society has always aspired.

We must remember that not until the individual has developed a respect for himself can he recognize and respect others, not until he has accepted himself, can he accept others. Not until each individual has a feeling of his own value and dignity will he be able to recognize and accept the value and worth of others.

If we will reflect on this situation, look more carefully at the conflicts and tensions, we will see, I believe, that a truly democratic social order is beginning to emerge and that all these conflicts and confusions would not exist unless it were beginning to emerge. We would also recognize perhaps more clearly that in so many different ways we are faced with the same basic problem of how to establish a social order dedicated to a recognition of the value of the individual. Is that not what we mean by the current discussion of social security and health care and better housing and improved industrial relations, of mental hygiene in education? In addition to the older belief in the equality of opportunity, we are now beginning to assert the urgent need of recognizing the equality of human needs as basic to the conservation of individual personalities.

This is a new and very difficult task because it means that we must assay all of our activities, in business, in industry, in trade, in government, in the professions, in education, and in religion, in terms of what they are doing to and for human personality and then endeavor to create new patterns for the conduct of human relationships and all these diverse activities and organizations. Thus, we are seeing the rise of new criteria both for individual conduct and for our social order. The further development and refining and ever-widening application of these criteria constitute the democratic task from now on.

It may be suggested, therefore, that this is the common ground we are trying to win, and as we go forward we must progressively reorganize almost every aspect and activity of our social order. Accordingly, we must say that it is a question, not merely of tolerating, but of encouraging diversities, recognizing the different cultural traditions and their meaning for different groups and likewise recognizing the idiomatic personality of individuals. We can build a unity around such diversities to the extent that we accept this common belief in the value of the individual and the equality of human needs and develop the patterns of nonexploitive, nondominating human relationships in all the varied activities of living.

When we clearly recognize the full meaning of this task we will become somewhat skeptical of the many formulas and plans and programs now being offered as remedies for our tensions and conflicts. In human relationships we must remember there are no substitutes for sincerity and generosity. This means that we can achieve this kind of unity with diversity only to the extent that we can increasingly become sane, emotionally balanced, integrated personalities who do not need to use or misuse others.

In approaching the problem of social order, let us always remember that it is not given, nor is it ever finally achieved. The answers we have proffered to the persistent tasks of life are shaped largely by the way we conceive these tasks and the problems and questions we pose. The quality of a social order, therefore, is to be judged primarily by what the members of that group recognize as problems and by the values and purposes which they are striving to achieve. Social order, in other words, is not given but is that which is sought.

In conclusion, it cannot be too strongly emphasized that if we desire a free, democratic social order, we must protect and develop each individual so that he is capable of carrying the burdens of freedom, of helping to maintain social order by self-discipline, co-operative conduct, and awareness of, and respect for, the personalities of others. We cannot, therefore, permit anyone, no matter how insignificant or seemingly unimportant he may seem, to be deprived, humiliated, degraded, terrorized, or otherwise damaged and distorted as a personality, because those so treated will be unable to participate in a free democratic society, incapable of developing the kind of human relationships required for achieving a free, unified social order.

PART TWO

THE DIVIDING ISSUES

IV

THE RACIAL ISSUE

BY

E. FRANKLIN FRAZIER

I

The problem of race relations in the modern world had its origin in the economic expansion of western Europe during the fifteenth and sixteenth centuries, which resulted not only in the spread of European culture but in the expansion of the white race. During the first three centuries of this expansion, the sparse settlements of whites in various parts of the world did not create a racial problem. The racial problem came into existence in the nineteenth century with the growth of large communities of whites in America and Africa and the extension of political control over most of Asia and virtually the entire continent of Africa. In America the racial and cultural frontiers, created by white settlement, were due as much to the importation of African slaves as to the presence of the indigenous race. In fact, in the West Indies and the United States, with which we are chiefly concerned, the racial problem is primarily the problem of the relations of whites and blacks. However, the problem of the relation of the white and colored races in the United States today is coming increasingly to involve the assimilation of 600,000 other colored people, about half of whom are American Indians.

Since this paper is concerned with the question of national unity and race relations, it is necessary to make clear that, despite recent attempts on the part of Aryan theorists to identify race and nation, the point of view of this paper is that the sentiment upon which national unity is based is not dependent upon racial identity. It is only when "racial differences enter into the consciousness of the individuals and groups so distinguished, and by so doing determine in each case the individual's conception of himself as well as his status in the community," [1] that race may be said to become a barrier to national unity. In the case of the Negro and the Oriental the visible racial marks have been chiefly responsible for their conception of themselves as a people apart and their status in the American community. But often these physical differences assume such importance in the minds of American thinkers that they have been regarded as insuperable barriers to assimilation. For example, Charles Francis Adams, in an address in 1908, declared that the American theory which assumed a "common humanity" and the "absence of absolutely fundamental racial characteristics" had broken down in regard to the African. "He remains," said Adams, "an alien element in the body politic. A foreign substance, he can neither be assimilated, nor thrown out." Therefore, the aim of this paper is to determine whether the Negro because of his physical characteristics will always remain an alien element or whether, in view of the changes in our American society and the Negro's changing relation to American life, there are grounds for believing that he may be integrated into our society and thereby contribute to national unity.

II

In the sense in which we are speaking of race relations, one may truthfully say that there was really no race problem in the South during the slavery period. African slaves were introduced into this country in order to supply certain definite labor needs for which some form of forced labor was required. Thus there was not during slavery any serious or open competition with white labor. Of course, as the number of the poorer nonslaveholding whites increased, there was a sort of impersonal competition. The real source of competition, however, came from the increasing number of free Negroes who acquired a monopoly on the mechanical arts in some of the cities of

[1] Robert E. Park, "The Nature of Race Relations," in *Race Relations and the Race Problem*. Edited by Edgar T. Thompson, Duke University Press, Durham, N.C., 1939, p. 3.

the South. To the extent that the poor whites regarded themselves as competitors of the free Negroes one might say that there was a race problem. In the same sense it is legitimate to say that a race problem existed in the North where there were constant conflicts between Negro and white workers, and the Negro had no place in either the economic or social organization.

On the other hand, in the South the great mass of the Negro population had not only a secure place in the economic organization but, as slavery acquired the character of a social institution, they became a part of the social organization. It was in the cities mainly where the free Negro population was concentrated that the colored population was outside the social organization. But this was not universally true, since in cities like Charleston, South Carolina, and New Orleans, the free Negro population, largely of mulatto origin, constituted an intermediate caste. In these two cities the social position of the members of this caste corresponded to their important function as skilled artisans in the economic organization. Moreover, the fact that this group was largely of mixed blood was indicative of the process of amalgamation that was slowed up as the result of the emancipation of the Negro. Although these mixbloods did not have the same status as mixbloods in Latin America, in many respects their emergence and social and economic position in Southern society represented a parallel development in race relations.

The Civil War and Reconstruction gave a new direction to race relations in the South and ushered in what has come to be known as the American race problem. Despite the heated controversies over the Reconstruction Period, we are beginning to revaluate the issues involved in the situation. It seems fairly well established that the Republican Party, which represented the triumph of northern industrialism over the semifeudalism of the South, was determined through the enfranchisement of the Negro to provide a legal basis for its victory. The support of Negro voters was secured by military force until there was sufficient political support from the Middle West to overcome opposition from the politically resurrected agricultural South. But these facts should not make us forget that a faction in the Republican Party was sincerely bent not only upon establishing the Negro as a free citizen but upon securing his freedom by making him and the poor white small landowners. However, in the end the Negro was left landless and as dependent as he had been in slavery. Moreover, he was deprived of his civil rights and received only a pittance of the educational and social services provided by southern communities. In fact, the South attempted through its Jim Crow legislation to establish what amounted to a caste system. During the period following Reconstruction race relations were characterized by considerable violence, which subsided only during the first decade of the present century. The new form of accommodation that emerged from this conflict and was accepted on the whole by Negroes and whites created a biracial organization in southern communities.

III

The migration of southern Negroes to northern cities during and following the First World War inaugurated a new stage in race relations in the United States. This does not mean simply that the race problem became national in scope. It means rather that the entire character of the problem was changed because the urbanized Negro acquired a new conception of himself, and the character of race relations was changed. In regard to race relations, the most important consequence of urbanization, in the South as well as in the North, was that the traditional relationship of loyalty and dependence upon whites was destroyed, and race consciousness and race loyalty have taken its place. As a part of this process the Negro has been able to escape, especially in the larger cities, from rigid caste restrictions. In fact, the movement to northern cities has really constituted a second emancipation for the Negro. It has broken down the social and mental isolation which has characterized the Negro communities of the South. A larger number of Negro children and youths have had access to the standard American education than at any time in the history of the Negro. As he has increased his literacy, he has gained access to a larger world of ideas. This process has been facilitated by the development during the past quarter of a century of Negro newspapers, several of which have a circulation of over 100,000. As the Negro has acquired new ideas, he has redefined the problem of his place in American life. At the same time he has been able to enjoy more civil rights and to exercise the right of suffrage and to hold office. Whereas in the rural South, social control has been most rigid in areas of Negro concentration, in the larger cities of the North, the Negro has exercised power because of his numbers.

These changes in the status and outlook of the Negro are related, of course, to the economic and social organization of our large cities. The migration of Negroes to the cities of the North was due initially to the increased demand for unskilled labor occasioned by the First World War and the cessation of foreign immigration. As the result of the migrations, the Negro was thus able to secure his first foothold in American industry. Although, when the great depression came in 1929, the insecurity of his position was revealed, he was not eliminated. However, partly because of his political power he was able to secure an equitable share of social services and benefits during the economic crisis. This did not solve the economic problems of the Negro in the northern city which continued to be critical, even when the economic revival set in as the result of the preparedness program. It was then that the Negro began to exhibit the new militancy for which the country was unprepared, because it was unaware of the changes that had taken place in the Negro and in his relation to American life during the past twenty-five years. This new militancy, which will increase in the future if his integration into American society is not facilitated, offers a serious threat to national unity.

IV

The pattern of race relations which grew out of the racial conflict following the fall of the Reconstruction governments in the South gave rise to the theory of a biracial organization as the solution of the race problem. According to this theory, as propounded at least by liberal southern whites, the Negro was to be given an opportunity for full development within a community framework separate from the white community. In order to preserve the purity of the white race—purity of the white race, since the Negro was already a highly mixed group—the two races were to carry on their lives within two separate sets of institutions. The liberal whites claimed that such an arrangement would work no injustice to the Negro, since he would have an opportunity for the fullest development of his capacities. Although the reactionary whites were determined upon inferior community facilities for the Negro as well as the separation of the races, the liberals hoped to bring them in time to the acceptance of the theory of "equality but separation."

The theory of a biracial organization was accepted, on the whole, by the leaders of the Negro group. In fact, the distinction which Booker T. Washington achieved as an interracial statesman was due to the fact that he not only provided the formula[2] for a biracial organization but utilized it, on the one hand, to stimulate the Negro to achieve through his own efforts and, on the other, to secure as much as possible for the Negro from the whites. Studiously avoiding such issues as the Negro's right to the franchise and the social relations of the two races, he sought larger support for a type of education which the South approved. Having convinced the North that he had found a solution of a problem of which the North was tired, he secured millions from northern philanthropists for private education. In 1900 he organized and became the first president of the National Negro Business League. This organization became largely responsible for the widely held belief among Negroes that their economic problems could be solved through the establishment of their own business and industrial enterprises. As a result, around the opening of the present century, there was a rather widespread belief among Negroes that despite the discrimination in the South, they could best work out their destiny there.

The theory of a biracial organization in which the two races could have opportunity for development was never achieved in practice. A biracial organization meant in practice the complete subordination of the Negro. By placing a stigma upon Negro blood, the South attempted to erect a caste system. The Negro was not only denied the right to vote, but he was denied justice in the courts; he became the

[2] "In all things that are purely social we can be as separate as the fingers, yet one as the hand in all things essential to mutual progress." Speech delivered at the opening of the Cotton States' Exposition, Atlanta, Georgia, Sept., 1895.

object of violence; he was held in peonage. He was denied employment in industry and received as a favor, but not as a right, a small fraction of the educational funds provided by the states. The so-called industrial education which the South approved officially did not prepare the Negro for participation in modern industry. Industrial education, which offered the Negro training in outmoded handicrafts, was acceptable because it symbolized the Negro's inferior position in society. As a matter of fact the Negro was completely excluded from employment in the cotton mills, which represented modern industry in the South.

When the theory of a biracial organization was first brought forward, four out of every five Negroes lived in the rural areas, and the majority of those in urban areas were in the smaller cities of the South. Consequently, there were some grounds for belief in the feasibility of a biracial organization. But during the present century, when over a million Negroes drifted into southern cities, it became apparent that the theory of a biracial organization did not present a solution for the race problem. The younger generation of Negroes recognized that the small enterprises owned by Negroes could not provide for the employment of Negroes. Moreover, it began to be generally recognized even by conservative Negro leaders in the South that, as long as there was disenfranchisement and a denial of civil rights, a biracial organization meant that the Negro would remain a pariah in southern society. Then came the mass migration of Negroes to northern industrial areas during and following the First World War which destroyed the belief that the Negro would work out his destiny in the South. The small intellectual Negro leadership in the North had never accepted the theory of a biracial organization. When the mass migrations created large communities of Negroes in the urban areas of the North, these leaders acquired a mass support for the demand that the Negro be integrated into American life. During the quarter of a century between our entrance into the First World War and the attack on Pearl Harbor, the Negro's new attitude toward his relation to American life was gaining acceptance among Negroes in the South as well as in the North. The present war with its emphasis upon the conflict between democratic and fascist ideologies has tended to destroy even more completely the traditional pattern of race relations and to create a nation-wide crisis in race relations.

v

The impossibility of a biracial organization as a solution of Negro-white relations is due primarily to the character of urban industrial society. In our large urban communities it would be impossible to enforce the caste barriers based upon racial descent which the South attempted to erect. It would immobilize the life of our cities. Even in the South, modern technology has made certain caste restrictions untenable in the interest of industrial efficiency. In regard to employment, it needs no demonstration to convince anyone that the Negro must be integrated into the industrial organization in order to survive. The integration of the Negro into industry means that the Negro must become a part of organized labor, and thus one cannot separate the "purely social" from other spheres of life. Moreover, one should not forget that with the rising standards of living which industrial employment and education create, the Negro cannot lead a full life within a segregated world. All of this simply means that a caste system or the more euphemistic term, a biracial organization, offers no solution of the racial problem in our modern urban industrial civilization.

This does not mean, of course, that the mere intellectual acceptance of this fact will eliminate the problems incident to the integration of the Negro into our society. There is still the problem of the Negro's physical appearance which tends to set him apart and to arouse antipathies. This is a factor that could not be ignored even if the majority of the American people were convinced that there were no important racial differences. Therefore, this factor should be faced first in any realistic discussion of the problem. In discussions of the color of the Negro and his integration into American life, the influence of social and cultural factors is generally ignored. There is always, at least implicit in most discussions, the position that color differences in themselves create repulsions or antipathies. In a certain sense this is true if we consider the attitudes of many northern whites or poor whites in the South. But if one considers the close association of the races in the South, especially before the Civil War, one will find that the physical quality of color is less important than the social fact of social status. Moreover, both in the North and in the South, the conception of the Negro or one might say the categoric picture of the Negro, is more influential in determining attitudes than the fact of physical color and features. The social visibility of the Negro is not simply his physical color but what one's conception of the Negro makes one see and feel when a Negro is present.

The fact of the Negro's physical characteristics should not be minimized, but it should not be regarded as an insuperable barrier to his integration into American life. In this connection one should bear in mind that a large proportion of Negroes are of mixed racial ancestry, and that they are often indistinguishable from whites. But what is of importance here is that the conception or categoric picture of the Negro has changed remarkably during the past twenty-five years. This change is perceptible first in pictorial representations. On the signboards and in advertisements, the Negro is no longer a caricature of a man. On the screen which provides an index to the public mind, the Negro is no longer a buffoon, and on the stage, at least in the more cosmopolitan centers, he has achieved the full stature of a normal human being. These changes in the conception of the Negro are not only indicative of changes in the status of the Negro in American life, but they are indicative of the changes which are taking place in the Negro. These changes are due in part to the fact that, in the competitive life of the city, some Negroes because of talent and education have been able to rise above the condition of the masses. Thus it is apparent that some of the problems of the Negro are not racial but problems incident to the adjustment of a peasant people to our urban civilization. If one would face frankly the problems of the integration of the Negro into our civilization, one must realize that the Negro is handicapped by his folk traditions. This has resulted in a considerable amount of social disorganization in Negro life. It has meant that the Negro family which was adapted to the folk culture of southern communities has failed in its function as a socializing agency. The importance of this fact cannot be overemphasized because of its importance in preparing the Negro to live in the city. At the same time the efficient functioning of the Negro family and the maintenance of a normal social life are conditioned by the restrictions placed upon the Negro because of his racial descent.

In exploring the possibilities of integrating the Negro into American society, it is necessary to consider some concrete problems of race relations. One of the constant sources of racial conflict has been the matter of the physical location of the two races or the problem of housing. After the First World War this was the real cause of the riot in Chicago, and it has been the cause of racial friction in several cities during the present war. From studies which have been made of the location of various racial and cultural groups in relation to the organization of our cities, there is no doubt that the relation of Negro communities is not due simply to racial prejudice or conscious attempts to restrict them to certain areas. There are impersonal economic and social factors which would create Negro communities, even if there were no prejudice against the Negro because of race. It is not, however, these impersonal economic and social factors which make housing a disturbing force in race relations. It is the attempt to confine the Negro to a ghetto that makes housing a source of constant racial conflict. In the Negro community, as in other communities, there is a tendency for the better situated economically and socially to move from the less desirable areas and from uncongenial neighbors. This normal process in the case of the Negro is prevented because it arouses fears of the invasion of Negro population. Yet in cities where this normal process has been able to operate there has been no wholesale invasion by Negroes simply because the white residents did not abandon their homes on account of the presence of one or two colored families. In neighborhoods where there has been a change to Negro occupancy on a large scale, the Negroes have entered because the neighborhood had already ceased to be a white residential area. The flight of white residents has always been not from the actual Negro residents but from the categoric picture of Negroes. There are numerous cases where white residents have remained and found the Negroes to be not only as desirable but more desirable than white neighbors. It is often a surprise to northern

whites to learn that Negroes and southern whites live in the same
neighborhoods, especially in the older cities.

As housing becomes a matter of public concern, the question of
the separate housing of Negroes has ushered in a new phase of the
problem. Unless one has a doctrinaire attitude toward social problems,
it presents a real problem for those who are sincere in their efforts to
integrate the Negro into the community. At the present time no sane
person would think of insisting that Negroes and whites occupy the
same housing units in the South. At the same time there is no excuse
for using the southern pattern for northern communities. If Negro
housing units are located in Negro areas in northern cities, they
would naturally be occupied by Negroes. If they are located in mixed
areas the proper policy is to accept white residents who are willing
to live in housing units with Negroes. In some northern cities Negroes
and whites are occupying the same housing facilities. The arrangements vary, but what is important is there is no attempt to stigmatize
the Negro by accepting the southern pattern of race relations. Unfortunately, the Federal Housing Authority has not simply attempted
to segregate the Negro, but it has designated him as an inharmonious
racial group to be excluded from new developments. Unless proper
provision is made for the integration of the Negro in the housing
plans for our communities, the housing of the Negro will continue
to be a source of serious racial conflicts.

It was around the issue of the integration of the Negro into our
industrial organization that the present crisis in race relations first
manifested itself. It was dramatized in the threatened "march on
Washington" in 1941, when the program of national defense failed
to make provision for Negro workers. This led to the issuance by the
President of the United States of the now famous Executive Order
8802, which reaffirmed the policy of nondiscrimination "because of
race, creed, color, or national origin" in government employment and
by contractors handling government orders. The Order also provided
for the setting up of a Committee of Fair Employment Practice to
carry out its purpose. The movement on the part of Negroes which
led to the issuance of the Order was significant because it indicated
the fundamental change that had taken place in the Negro's atti-

tude toward his problem as the result of urbanization. The Order itself was even more significant since it marked the abandonment of the *laissez-faire* policy of the Federal Government in regard to the relation of the Negro to our economic organization. This change in policy was undoubtedly related to the growing control of the government over the economic process during the war, but the fact that both parties in the election just past pledged their support of the Committee of Fair Employment Practice indicates that those in control of federal legislation recognize that something must be done to remove or modify caste practice in our economic system.

During the period of its operation, the F.E.P.C. has not succeeded in removing discriminations in the employment of Negroes. It has succeeded to some extent in removing the barriers against Negroes in the war industries. Discrimination against Negroes, it should be noted, is due to the attitude of white workers, both organized and unorganized, as well as to the employment policies of employers. The opposition of organized white workers is due chiefly to the traditional policies of the unions in the American Federation of Labor. On the other hand, the unions which form the Congress of Industrial Organizations have in their practices outside of the South approximated their official policy of nondiscrimination. In fact, it might be said that not until the C.I.O. was organized did unions offer any advantages to Negro workers. The success which the F.E.P.C. has achieved is related to this development in the American labor movement during recent years. The new development coincided with the inauguration and operation of the National Labor Relations Act which guarantees certain rights to labor. Thus the protection of the rights of the Negro to equal opportunity in the economic life is tied up with governmental policy in regard to labor. In view of the position of the American Federation of Labor and the attitude of Congress, it is doubtful that the government will take drastic steps to abolish racial discrimination in employment. There is more hope in the growing disposition on the part of most unions to provide greater participation for the Negro workers on terms of equality. On the other hand, where the unions depend for their power and control of labor upon federal protection, public opinion must be organized to protect the Negro in his right to work.

As one views the outlook for the Negro worker in the postwar world, there are indications that racial conflict in the field of employment may cause serious threats to national unity. In the conversion of war industries to production for civilian needs, Negro workers will suffer more than white workers, since they have not secured a foothold in those industries, both new and old, that will provide for peacetime needs. Even if discharges are based upon seniority, the fact that the Negro has only recently entered industry will operate to his disadvantage. Moreover, the demobilization of the Negroes in the Armed Forces will throw a larger number upon the labor market. These men will be less disposed than Negroes in the past to remain unemployed because of race, nor will they be satisfied to be shunted into the precarious employment afforded by unskilled labor. Their war experiences as well as the sophistication afforded by city life will dispose them to make common cause with the radical and dissident forces in American life. One may expect an intensification of race consciousness which will result in the type of racial chauvinism that characterized the Garvey Movement after the First World War. Perhaps, many more will be drawn into the radical wing of the labor movement and seek a revolutionary solution of their problem. At one time such movements on the part of the Negro could be ignored, but in our urban civilization they offer a serious threat to internal peace. Since the employment of the Negro cannot be separated from the problem of full employment, the integration of the Negro into industry will depend largely upon whether we can run our productive machinery at full capacity. But even under favorable conditions it will be necessary to provide for the participation of the Negro worker on the same terms as other workers. If the Federal Government fails to pass measures to deal with this problem, then the northern states will have to make some provisions to prevent racial strife in industrial areas.

The third area in which problems of integration are becoming acute concerns political and civil rights. This is especially true of race relationships in the South. Despite the Constitution and the ruling of the Supreme Court, in some parts of the South there is a determination, even if it involves violence, to prevent the Negro from exercising the right of the franchise. In other areas, especially where the Negro forms a smaller proportion of the population, there is a growing disposition to permit the Negro to vote on the same terms as whites. One of the arguments advanced in defense of the disfranchisement of the Negro is that he is ignorant and lacks the political education and traditions to enjoy the rights of democratic citizenship. As the Negro is acquiring literacy and the general cultural level of the Negro population is rising, this argument is losing force. The second argument against permitting the Negro to vote concerns the matter of white supremacy. It is argued that if the Negro votes, there will be Negro domination in some areas and a recurrence of all the evils of Reconstruction. This argument, it will be noted, rests partly upon the myth of Negro domination during the Reconstruction. Fortunately, this myth is being dissipated through the dissemination of the results of unbiased historical research. Moreover, there is a growing number of southern whites who are getting a more realistic view of the question of Negro domination at the present time. The fear of Negro domination is subsiding partly because there is no longer any state in the South where Negroes outnumber whites. But, in addition, whites are beginning to realize that the divergence of interests among Negroes, which is assuming considerable importance with the social and economic differentiation of the Negro population, will preclude any organized political solidarity against the whites. Thus the only reasonable course which the South should pursue is to integrate the Negro into its political organization on the same terms as the whites.

If this were accomplished, the problem of civil rights would still remain to be solved. It is conceivable, of course, that this problem would become more acute if political rights were granted, since the Negro could enforce the recognition of his civil rights. The enjoyment of equal civil rights involves the relation of the races on railroads, buses, and other means of transportation and in the use of public institutions. It has been in this area of race relations that the principle of caste has been most rigid. Despite the rationalizations concerning the Negro's lack of cleanliness and uncouth behavior, which are used to support the separation of the races, it is obvious that its main purpose is to maintain the Negro in an inferior status. In the matter of public institutions it is apparent that the Negro's economic and social position will determine which he will patronize and to what extent he will patronize them, just as in the use of the Pullman car today. But the difficulty in the mind of the white South is that it fails to recognize that many relations which were private or semiprivate in a rural society are public in an urban society. However, that there is a growing recognition that Jim Crow transportation is not necessary, is indicated by the proposal of the editor of a leading Virginia paper to abolish this form of segregation. It is also worth noting that despite the Jim Crow law, Negro and white passengers are riding together without conflict in northern Virginia because of the heavy travel incident to the recent war.

Although the Negro enjoys full political equality in the North, the denial of civil rights remains a source of racial conflict. The denial of civil rights in the North does not have the same historical and traditional background as in the South. It is more arbitrary and unpredictable; it is due more to individual antipathies and whims. At the same time certain stereotyped notions and conceptions of the Negro play a role. In some areas, the exclusion of the Negro from public institutions is, of course, supported by public opinion. But, on the whole, in the North the civil rights of the Negro can be guaranteed by the enforcement of the law. Therefore, as these stereotyped notions are dissipated through education in a broad sense and the social visibility of the Negro decreases, there should be less racial conflict in the area of civil rights. Of course, the social visibility of the Negro is increased by his ignorance of city ways, by his poverty, by other indications of lower-class status.

A discussion of the civil rights of the Negro leads inevitably to the question of the integration of the Negro into those phases of the social organization involving the more intimate relations between men. In the South, the general feeling even among liberal whites is that certain barriers which prevent the Negro from enjoying civil rights are justified because they prevent a type of association that will lead to intermarriage and amalgamation. It is needless to argue that the Southern attitude is illogical and unscientific, since racial mixture was carried on on a large scale in the South as long as the Negro was a slave and since there is no evidence that the mixed blood is inferior to either of the parent stocks. Many enlightened men in the South acknowledge these facts. But they regard them as irrelevant to the situation in the South. Some southern liberals are beginning to talk, however, of the cultural integration of the Negro into Southern society in so far as it does not threaten the racial integrity of the white race. Although it is difficult to see how cultural integration will be possible as long as there is a stigma upon Negro blood, such a position indicates a growing recognition of the fact that a completely segregated biracial organization is impossible.

In the North where social distances are maintained in regard to the more intimate association of the two races, there is on the whole no deep-seated fear that civil and political equality will break down such barriers. At the same time, there is not only a general aversion to intermarriage, but there are also barriers to the association of whites and Negroes in common activities where the so-called purely social relations are involved. These caste practices are not only incompatible with the spirit of an urban society based upon democracy but must be eliminated if racial peace is to be achieved. Mainly because of these economic and civil discriminations, we have the phenomenon of "passing" for white on the part of Negroes of mixed ancestry. In fact, it is through the process of "passing" that many Negroes are becoming integrated into the social organization, though they lose their identity as Negroes. This process will continue as long as a stigma is placed upon Negro blood. Though the infiltration of white blood into the Negro group has slowed up during the past fifty years, it is likely that it will increase in our cities, especially since other minority groups do not have the same aversion to intermarriage as the old American stocks. In order to remove the threat of race to national unity, the feeling of color caste and the fiction of a pure white race must be abandoned.

In summing up this discussion of the relation of the racial issue to the achievement of national unity, it is possible to draw certain fairly clear conclusions. First, the theory of a biracial organization as a solution of the racial problem is untenable. The relations which developed in a rural society provided some basis for the belief in such a solution. In practice, the biracial organization turned out to be essentially a caste system in which the Negro was subordinated and the democratic theory was repudiated. Second, in our highly mobile urban civilization, a biracial organization or a caste system is not only impossible but leads to racial conflicts on a scale that threatens national unity. Third, the integration of the Negro into our economic, political, and social organization becomes a necessity. That such integration is feasible is demonstrated by the integration of the Negro into the Armed Forces, especially into those branches where the caste principle was most rigid. Any other policy will cause the Negro to ally himself as a racial minority with revolutionary and dissident forces in American life and thus become a serious threat to national unity.

V

THE ETHNIC ISSUE

BY

VILHJALMUR STEFANSSON

There is no time for preliminaries and I plunge into the topic by telling a story for which I cannot vouch except that I know it is true in principle. A friend of mine who is a student of colonial history, particularly that of New England, told me a few years ago that the incident I am about to speak of had not, so far as he knew, been published; but he had seen old records from which he got the story.

It seems that the Pilgrims and others in the region of Massachusetts considered that there were many remarkable differences between themselves and the Indians; one which clearly indicated a profound difference was that white children needed to learn to swim, but that Indian children, like animals, could instinctively swim. A boatload of these early New Englanders was crossing a bay. They met an Indian woman in a canoe with her two children. This seemed to them a good opportunity to try out the theory, and they tipped over the canoe. They found that the theory in which they had previously believed was incorrect, for these children were unable to swim and were drowned. Whereupon they considered it to be established that while the Indians differed from other people in many respects, they did not differ in this respect; they would have to learn to swim the same as the Puritans.

This story is unfortunately typical of our ethnic history. The first contact we know between Europeans and the North American Indians occurred in Labrador. A little farther south, in the Gulf of St. Lawrence, probably, the Norsemen, who were trying to colonize what they called "Wineland," met some exceptionally intelligent and foresighted natives who drove them off in time. On their way back along the coast of Labrador, in their retreat toward Greenland, these Scandinavians came upon some natives of an entirely different people; that is, people many hundreds of miles away from where the battle had occurred from which they had concluded they had better return to Greenland. These people were sleeping in the shelter of a boat and they killed them in their sleep.

I was born in Manitoba, but our family moved south into the Territory of Dakota, and I was brought up among people who were not thinking they were funny when they said, "The only good Indian is a dead Indian."

We speak with pride of our conquest of this continent. The conquest began, generally speaking, by our first landing here and there along the Atlantic coast in small, weak numbers, groups of us. While we were weak, we got help from the Indians; when we became strong enough, we began to take their land away from them, and if they demurred we drove them out by force of arms. It did not occur to us, apparently, that we were doing anything wrong. It was this attitude which the farmers in my own community had later toward the buffalo. The buffalo cumbered the land which the farmer wanted to use for hay fields and wheat fields and the grazing of domestic cattle; so they slaughtered the buffalo, partly, of course, to be able to sell the skin, but partly just to get them out of the way.

This attitude toward the native American has been so vividly preserved that even now there is tremendous excitement in the Territory of Alaska over what was described in the Alaska newspapers as the "Ickes land grab." The papers said that Ickes, Secretary of the Interior, had an iniquitous plan to grab Alaska land away from the people to whom it belongs, and the people to whom it belongs, according to the Alaska view, are the miners and other squatters who are sprinkled here and there throughout the territory. It has not occurred to the white Alaskans, seemingly, that the forest Indians of Alaska and the prairie Eskimos have rights, and that the "Ickes land grab" was an attempt by the Department of the Interior to preserve some of Alaska for the use of its native people.

Yesterday the *Herald-Tribune* (November 27, 1944), at the liberality of which, as a Republican paper, I am sometimes astonished, contained an editorial captioned, "An Indian for President." The first sentence read: "The statement of Mr. John Collier, Commissioner of Indian affairs, that there is no reason why an Indian should not be President of the United States probably will be widely spoofed by commentators to whom the idea of an American Indian holding this office is, *per se,* ludicrous."

This noon—I am bringing this down to date—I was on my way to this meeting by the subway, and I read in the *New York Post* of November 28 an article by Edgar Ansell Mowrer condemning certain things which all of us dislike about the Germans. He speaks of them as conducting themselves in such a way that they are not entitled to the protection of international law, particularly the international law governing war. In this argument he says of the Germans: "They have no more rights than a band of Cherokee Indians."

There are few things that Hitler has done to the Jew or to the democrat or to the Communist that he might not have taken from the book of the history of the continent of North America. When the Corte-Real brothers, possibly a year or two before Cabot—some claim even before Columbus—landed on the coast of North America, probably somewhere in the Labrador or Newfoundland section, they took prisoners and carried them back to Portugal. They captured some natives and took them back home to show them off and then to sell them. One of the first plans that Columbus made for the New World was for the enslavement of the Indians.

In this brief talk I naturally have not the time to canvass the whole story, and I come to the main point I want to make, which can be exemplified from the study of one people, the Eskimos: They are being treated in distinct and in some respects very different ways by four governments. The Danes in Greenland have one method, the Canadians and the United States in northern Canada and Alaska have another method, the Soviet government over in Siberia have a third method.

There are in Greenland about twenty thousand Eskimos. They were dying off rapidly until the Danish government assumed toward them an efficiently benevolent attitude. They are treated as wards,

which the Danish government understands to mean, among other
things, that they are to be kept alive. The Danes never had the idea,
apparently, that the only good Indian is a dead Indian; so they quar-
antined the country—that was, of course, before the war—so that
Greenland was a more isolated country than Tibet, the most isolated
country in the world. No tourist could go there unless he were carefully disguised. A few tourists did get there, but always by pretend-
ing they were something else. You could not go to a travel agency and
say, "I want a ticket for Greenland." What you would do was to
figure out that you were an artist, a scientist, a historian, someone of
that sort. You would apply to our State Department saying, for instance, "I am a portrait painter; I specialize in the painting of the
aborigines of North America and desire permission to visit Greenland
to make studies and to paint portraits." Then our State Department,
acting through its minister in Copenhagen, would apply to the Danish government and you would undoubtedly get the permission.
Some variant of this process had to be used, or you would not get into
Greenland.

A result of these and other features of Danish policy was that the
people increased in numbers. The Danes wanted the Greenland
Eskimos to preserve their economic independence and their self-
respect; so they encouraged them to sew their own clothing and to
live extensively on their own food. They stationed well-trained medical men at suitable intervals along the coast who visited all the settlements. They provided for the education of the Eskimos *in the Eskimo
language*. That is a very important point; for it is almost impossible,
as we find in Alaska, to educate people in a foreign tongue. When you
try to teach in an Eskimo village using the English language, "you
succeed in attaining failure." If you teach in the Eskimo language,
success is easier. I know this from my own experience. I have taught
the alphabet to Eskimos who had no conception previously that
there could be an alphabet, and I have come back two or three
years later to find nearly everybody in the village reading and writing.
Knowledge spreads like the measles when it is in the native tongue
but spreads with difficulty in a foreign tongue. The Danes in Green-

land teach Danish, but only as a foreign language, as we teach French, and many Eskimos learn it.

Let me pass on to Canada and Alaska. The theory is that the Eskimos are the wards of our two governments; but in practice we give them little care or protection. In the Canadian Arctic there has never been any attempt at quarantine, and there are no physicians stationed throughout the North, except that in a few Royal Canadian Mounted Police posts there are surgeons who belong to the police and who will treat Eskimos in those immediate vicinities.

One result of this has been that while the Eskimo population in Greenland was increasing, the Canadian Eskimo population has been going down so that between Labrador and Canada, in that vast country, there are now less than nine thousand Eskimos. There were probably at least two hundred thousand in those same territories before white men's diseases and the white man's general way of life were introduced.

In Alaska the condition is a little better. The Canadians do nothing for the education of the Eskimos except to give a small subsidy to church schools, usually Roman Catholic or Anglican. The main concern in these schools is the inculcation of religion, which is mainly done in English or in French. Here and there, both among the Roman Catholics and the Anglicans, you will find a missionary who does not believe in the general practice and who personally and individually tries to teach in the Eskimo language. But the general system is to teach in English except in a few places where they teach in French. It is the Roman Catholics, not the Anglicans, who teach in French, usually.

For more than twenty thousand Eskimos in Alaska the United States government has sent in some schoolteachers but they teach in English. They have sent in a few medical men. The Eskimos are protected against a few things, chiefly against drink. They are very ingenious people and they very soon learn to make home brew, to make moonshine alcohol. The police and other authorities go around and try to stop this. That is almost the only protection the Alaska Eskimos get, except in the regular police way, from criminals.

Bound for the Soviet Union, we now cross Bering Straits, fifty-six miles wide. There are two islands near the middle, so that no gap is wider than the English Channel. The territories of the Soviet Union and the United States are less than three miles apart; in winter the Eskimo school children of our Little Diomede and of their Big Diomede visit back and forth, walking across landfast sea ice. In one school are pictures of Roosevelt and Wallace and the teaching is in English; in the other school the pictures are of Stalin and Molotov and the teaching is in Eskimo. The Soviet Union has actually gone much farther than the Danes in that respect, for Dane-supported Eskimo books usually treat of Christians and other non-Greenlandic matters. The Soviets have printed beautiful books in the Eskimo language, I think in Leningrad, possibly in Moscow, which are written from the Eskimo point of view, with illustrations in the primary books of reindeer, polar bears, dogsleds and things that the people are familiar with. Later on, of course, in the higher years they get books that tell about the outside world, but in the first few years it is their own country that is described.

In Greenland the Danes say to the Eskimos, "You are like children; we will protect you." And they do protect the Eskimos. They protect them, for instance, against gasoline. They have decided that it is safe to entrust the Eskimo, considering his grade of intelligence, with kerosene, but that it is not safe to entrust him with gasoline; an Eskimo may own a power boat, but only a heavy-oil-driven power boat; he may not own a gasoline-driven power boat. In Canada an Eskimo may own anything he can buy, and that is also true in Alaska.

By contrast with Greenland, Canada, and Alaska, the Soviet authorities have said to the Eskimos, "You are ordinary Soviet citizens; you are neither better nor worse than anybody else." They told them, "You are to organize a Soviet." Of course, the Eskimos had no idea what a Soviet was; they were told what it was and they were made to organize Soviets. They selected their brightest children, who were sent to school outside to learn arithmetic, world history, Marxism, and the rest.

I can never find out how many racial or national groups there are in the Soviet Union. The last book I read said there were one hundred and eighty-nine. I sat next to a Soviet official the other night and he said there are more than one hundred. Eskimos are simply one group of one hundred, or one of one hundred and eighty-nine.

Many travelers from Greenland, Labrador, Northern Canada, and Alaska have said that the Eskimo is mechanically the most ingenious person they ever saw. For instance, we have stories that come from centuries apart in time and thousands of miles apart in distance, which tell how an Eskimo will purchase or receive as a gift a watch. The watch will run for a while; when it stops this man who has never seen a watch before will take it apart and clean it and, if there is a part broken, he will very often repair it. For instance, if he has another watch that is broken down he will take a piece from the other watch and move it to his watch.

Stories of the degree of Eskimo mechanical ability would be incredible if they were not so numerous and from so many different times and places.

In Canada one or two Eskimos, possibly more, have been used as assistant mechanics by aviators in the far North. Aviation, of course, is the great method of transportation in the North everywhere, in the Soviet Union, Alaska, Canada, and now Greenland. In Alaska, when the present war began, there was one forest Indian girl who had taken a few flights with the idea of possibly becoming a pilot. When we received the last news out of the Eskimo part of the Soviet Union, in 1939, there were already six Eskimos out of their twelve hundred who were accredited pilots, one of them with one hundred and seventy solo hours, as against the Alaskan unit where there was not a single Eskimo pilot out of more than twenty thousand. They consider in the Soviet Union that the Eskimo has the same average ability as a Russian or a Georgian or a Uzbek or any of the other nationalities.

I was recently told over again what I had heard before, that Stalin is as much an author of the Soviet nationalities' doctrine as, say, Jefferson is the author of the Declaration of Independence, meaning, of course, that Jefferson was not completely the author, but that it is not incorrect to speak of him in that relation. They have carried out the principle of the equalities of nationalities and races in every respect, including nomenclature. Nomenclature, by the way, seems to me important. There were people in Imperial Russia called Samoyeds, which means cannibals. Now it is a part of Soviet law that no people may be called by any name which they do not themselves approve; and so, in the Russian language books in my library, when I want to look up the Samoyeds, I look for Nenets. I would perhaps find on the first page of the discussion an asterisk after the name Nenets, and there would be a footnote saying these are the people that were formerly called Samoyeds.

In our country we have the opposite method. We call the Mexicans "greaser"; we call an Indian man a "buck," we call his wife a "squaw," and we call his child a "papoose," all with implications which humiliate and irritate and anger the people to whom they are applied.

We have all noticed that in the Soviet Union they are extremely careful not to speak of Russia unless they mean Russia! As in the British commonwealth of nations people are careful not to say England if they mean Britain or United Kingdom.

This precision of terminology was well illustrated the other night. At a speechmaking dinner I sat beside the Soviet Ambassador, Mr. Gromyko. When his talk was over, I asked him for a copy of a passage from his speech because I wanted to be able to quote correctly his use of certain nationalistic and racial terms. He gave me his whole speech; I have it here. I will read you one or two sentences:

"The Jews are absolutely equal members of the great family of citizens of the Soviet Union. They work, fight, and they die for the Motherland just as do the Russians, the Ukrainians, the Byelo Russians, the Georgians, the Armenians, the Uzbeks, and the others."

It is perhaps a minor point, but one I want to commend to your attention, that, when we call ourselves Americans, we irritate all the Latin-American nations. When Professor MacIver and I first met in Canada, about twenty-five years ago, Canadians were still annoyed when we from the States called ourselves Americans. Some of them claim now they are so proud of being Canadians that they are glad we call ourselves Americans. They make out they are avoiding an implied slur by calling themselves Canadians. But I think that really Canadians are still a bit annoyed; certainly the Latin-Americans are annoyed. It appears to me to be one of the important minor points in our racial relations that we shall say Negro in place of "nigger," that we shall speak of Indian women as women and not as "squaws," of the Mexicans as Mexicans rather than "greasers." If only it were feasible it would be a good thing to stop calling ourselves Americans, as if we were the only ones or at least the best ones.

Last spring I read in a paper that a high-school boy, a very good baseball player, could not play on the team of his high school in New Mexico because he was of Mexican ancestry. His grandparents had come over, and he had been in our country, on our side of the Rio Grande, for three generations. Yet he was still a "greaser" and could not play on the team.

We have done extremely well in the Philippines and the Filipinos have supported us as no people of Asia have supported the Dutch, or the Netherlanders, I should say; I must be a little careful myself. Colonel Romulo, now General Romulo, of the Philippine government, is a friend of mine. He read in the papers, as you did, that Filipino soldiers in California, on weekends, when they went to town wearing the uniform of Uncle Sam, could not walk up to a soda counter to buy a soda, not an ordinary soda counter; they would have to have separate ones. They could not register for rooms in a hotel, they could not sit down in a restaurant to a meal. Colonel Romulo tells me he hopes to be among the first to go back to the Philippines to explain to his people as best he can that we are pretty nice in the United States in spite of all this; but he is afraid that much of the admiration and gratitude of the Filipinos for how fine we have been in the Philippines is going to be obliterated when their own soldiers return from our country and report how they were treated.

DISCUSSION

QUESTION: What may we call ourselves that will not be taken amiss by other people—we people of the United States?

MR. STEFANSSON: We could call ourselves the United States of America, which I believe is our official title, or we could call ourselves the United States of North America, which would perhaps be precise. In the war between the States the Northerners called themselves Unionists. The difficulty is a serious one; but if we are going to get along well with other nations we must remove as many handicaps as we can; and one of the handicaps to remove, if possible, especially in our relations with Latin-America, is this arrogance of calling ourselves Americans.

QUESTION: Who are the Uzbeks?

MR. STEFANSSON: I believe they are in the South Central part, but I am not sure. There are some people here from the Soviet Union. Will somebody answer for me just where the Uzbeks are? I was merely reading a paragraph from the speech of the Ambassador.

ANSWER FROM THE AUDIENCE: They are near Georgia. You find most of them near Georgia. They are in the hills in Georgia, too, in the Caucasus. Many of them are shepherds in the Caucasus.

QUESTION: Is there a common language for the Eskimos in Greenland, for instance, and Alaska?

MR. STEFANSSON: Yes; the difference between Eskimo spoken on the east coast of Greenland and Eskimo spoken on the west coast of Alaska is no greater than between Spanish and Portuguese. It actually occurred that an Eskimo came from Greenland to Point Barrow and could not understand a word the day he landed there from a ship; but a week later, he told me, he understood every word. It was chiefly a matter of getting used to the pronunciation; but, of course, there were a few new words, a very few. There are many dialects in the Eskimo language but the language is one.

QUESTION: To what extent have the Eskimos developed a literature of their own?

MR. STEFANSSON: In quantity they have a tremendous literature. As to quality, that is rather difficult for us to judge because the Eskimo language is probably the most difficult language on earth to learn. I was a fairly good linguist, considered so in college; I had a reading knowledge of ten languages before I went north and I spoke two fluently. I went to work hard on the Eskimo language. I had a good Eskimo grammar from Greenland, a very good dictionary from Greenland, just as useful to me as if they had been a local grammar and a local dictionary. At the end of a year of intense application, living in the homes of the Eskimos, I could hardly speak a word. On my second expedition it was at the end of my fourth year in the Arctic, ninety per cent of the time within hearing of Eskimo being spoken, always working at it—it was only toward the end of my fourth year that suddenly a command of the language came to me in the course of a month or two. I found myself then able to speak Eskimo as fluently as English, but of course with a pronounced accent. So, since the language is almost unlearnable to us, we cannot very well judge of the quality of its literature.

Stories are memorized. When they are being told, everybody sits quiet; they are working at skins or something, but noiselessly. If the narrator, who has been selected because of ability as a narrator, says anything that is wrong, they wait until there is a pause—he speaks very slowly—and then someone will speak up and say, "Now, doubtless you are right on this point; but if I remember correctly, in this very room four years ago, when your uncle, who unfortunately has since died, told this story, he told it a little differently, and this is how I think he told it."

The critic then gives his version. The narrator does not say a word. Others chip in, one of whom may say, "I was there too and I agree that the narrator is a little off; but I don't quite agree with his critics either."

They will discuss the point for half an hour, or maybe for an entire evening. Finally they will arrive at an informal conclusion, a vote you might say, on the correct version. Then the narrator, if he has been over-ruled, will go back a little in his story and tell it again, this time being careful to bring out the point in accord with the decision of the audience.

So you see, an Eskimo's appreciation of a story is very much like a musician's appreciation of music. Students of music, even great musicians, will go to hear other musicians mainly to study the little variations. When we see Hamlet, what is in our minds may well be chiefly a comparison of the Hamlet that is before us with other Hamlets whom we remember. That is the Eskimo audience's attitude to stories.

There are classics, stories that are almost as well known to the audience as to the narrator. Eskimos tell new stories, too. In a new story you do not have to be so careful as to how you tell it; with an old story you have to be very careful. There are millions and millions of words of these stories.

QUESTION: May I ask further whether we are translating some of our own classics into their literature?

MR. STEFANSSON: I suppose the Bible is a classic. It has been translated into many Eskimo dialects. I think the more important thing is to translate their stories into our language, instead of this constant passion to teach everybody about us, we should realize the importance of learning about other peoples. Something along that line has been done; I have done some of it myself. I have published very little Eskimo folklore, but I have perhaps a hundred thousand words of unpublished translation.

I find, incidentally, when I copy down Eskimo on my typewriter from slow narration and then translate it into idiomatic English, that one page of Eskimo makes about two-and-one-half pages of English. It is a very condensed, concise, and precise language, a very good language.

The interesting thing about a language is how it is constructed. Since there is not time to explain this, I will say that it belongs to the same family as Magyar. There is probably somebody in this room who speaks Magyar or, if not, who has a friend who does. The Magyar language—also Finnish and Lappish—belongs to the same family as Eskimo. While it took me four or five years to learn Eskimo, a Finn can learn Eskimo in a few months because the structure of the two languages is essentially the same.

QUESTION: How long have they had a written language?

MR. STEFANSSON: The Eskimos, like the English or the French, have borrowed their alphabet from other people. Eskimo, in appreciable quantity and with fair quality of scholarship, was first written down by the Danish missionary Hans Egede shortly after 1721, which is the year he arrived in Greenland; so that is how long they have had the alphabet. I myself introduced the alphabet at the mouth of the Mackenzie River in 1906. There are other districts where it has been introduced more recently. The Greenlanders are the only ones who publish extensively in their own language. There is a magazine, or rather an annual, which was first published in 1863 and which is still being published. Every contributor, printer, subscription solicitor is an Eskimo. So an Eskimo journal is now one of the older—not the oldest, but one of the older—journals of North America.

QUESTION: May I ask a question dealing with the first part of your address? You started as a preacher and you cannot quite escape it. You raised a very challenging point. You implied that there was something morally wrong in the white man's coming and taking the territory from the Indian—taking the continent from the Indian.

Do you mean to say that it was morally wrong (I ask that not as an academic question, but for the future) for a group needing territory insisting on settling in a territory that is already settled? Or do you mean to say that "finders, keepers" applies to territory as well as to oil wells, or do you challenge oil wells on the same theory too, or what?

MR. STEFANSSON: I did not really mean to do anything more than to bring out the parallel. We felt the need for additional room and instead of taking it from the Poles and the Ukrainians, we decided to take it from the North American Indians. I was rather drawing a parallel. I would go no further than to say that, if Hitler was wrong, it seems to me we were equally wrong.

QUESTION: Are the North American Eskimos antagonistic to our government? Are the Siberian Eskimos sympathetic with the Soviet?

MR. STEFANSSON: No, the Eskimos are nowhere antagonistic. They are communistic anarchists and their fundamental principle of ethics is to get along with everybody. The worst crime among the primitive Eskimo is troublemaking. For instance, if I am a liar and if you go around saying quite truthfully that I am a liar, you are the worse of the two of us, because you are stirring up trouble. Among the Eskimos formerly, a person who kept on stirring up trouble long enough was eventually executed. He was to be executed by his nearest of kin. That is the Eskimo theory, that a man should not be executed until his nearest of kin have been convinced that he is an incurable troublemaker; then they are supposed to execute him. This does not always prevent the outbreak of a blood feud.

On the whole Eskimos are the most amenable people you can imagine. For instance, if I say to an Eskimo: "I hope the weather will be good tomorrow, we are going on a picnic," then the only correct answer for him is to agree. It is extremely difficult to get unbiased evidence out of an Eskimo. You have to make it perfectly clear to him that you do not care at all which way the evidence goes, otherwise he will give you only his best guess at what you would like to hear. We understand this in a way and call it a white lie. It is like our visiting a friend who is in bed in the hospital and saying, "You are looking fine today." He may not be looking fine, but that is what we are supposed to say.

The Eskimos are very easy to get along with. The Danes, the Canadians, and we have found them so. The Soviet government has found them so.

QUESTION: I want to ask about the narrators: Do they travel about from place to place widely?

MR. STEFANSSON: A man who is well known to be a good narrator is levied upon if he happens to be passing through. They do not travel on purpose to tell stories. The community changes from year to year. If there are ten inhabited houses in a village, it is rare to find more than five of them occupied this year by the same families who occupied them a year ago. Those families have gone to other communities and other families have come in in their place.

QUESTION: How wide is the difference between the Cherokee and the Eskimo? I was wondering how it would go with the plains Indians, the Indians of your part of the country, the Blackfeet or Sioux, or any of those?

MR. STEFANSSON: In my view the Eskimos are just one kind of Indian so I would rather expect that there would be a linguistic similarity.

QUESTION: You say they are probably Indians and yet you say, linguistically, they seem to be more connected with the Finns and the Magyars.

MR. STEFANSSON: I would have thought there would be other Indians, besides the Eskimos, whose language would be structurally connected with the Finns and the Magyars.

QUESTION: Are they not the latest comers from the Asiatic continent and therefore connected with the Japanese and Finns and Magyars?

MR. STEFANSSON: So far as I know, they are not linguistically connected with the Japanese. As to the Eskimos being the latest comers, that has been a common belief; but a friend of mine in Canada threatens to publish a book any minute to prove they are not the latest comers, that the Athabascan Indians came later; but I think even Marius Barbeau would say they are second last, if not last. I think they have been here only about three thousand years or so.

QUESTION: Is there a bond that unifies these people, either philosophically or religiously?

MR. STEFANSSON: They have a common religious outlook. For instance, none of them have, in my opinion, any conception similar to our idea of a God, nothing like our Devil, nothing like our Hell, they do not have good spirits and evil spirits, except on the frontier where they are in close touch with other people, where they have, perhaps, borrowed the idea of good spirits and evil spirits from forest Indians or whites.

So far as I can analyze the Eskimo—what you might call the authentic Eskimo belief—they think of the spirits as powerful, somewhat as we think of electricity or gunpowder as being powerful. They think every spirit is under the control of a *shaman,* or at least is potentially so; the spirit will do the good or evil bidding of the *shaman.* It is not a good spirit or evil spirit in itself. The Eskimos have no chiefs and so they do not have a God that resembles an earthly chief or king.

Their spirits vary in power; they arrive at the power of the spirit by observation. Suppose two of us are *shamans.* You have a "polar bear" spirit and I have a "red fox" spirit. We are called in to treat various cases of illness. If I am more successful through the aid of my red fox than you are through the aid of your polar bear, the feeling will gradually grow that my red fox is more powerful than your polar bear. However, that does not mean that somebody else's red fox spirit, which is a different one, may not be less powerful than mine; or it may be twice as powerful. This is just the sort of thinking you would expect from a primitive people who are communistic anarchist.

THE CHAIRMAN: You could sit around these tables for a long time and Mr. Stefansson's stories would get better and better all the time, you can take it from me, but it is past our time now. So merely in thanking Mr. Stefansson for his extremely interesting talk, I would like to point the lesson in one small way:

You will notice that every speaker who comes, each with his different angle, adds something more to our store of knowledge, of what it means to have groups together, races together, in the same community, and what it means if you treat them one way and what it means if you treat them another way.

We are learning—at least we should be learning—how much we lose by treating them the other way. The lesson is being driven home to us directly and indirectly all the time.

We are, of course, the most multigroup country in the world. The Soviet Union may have its hundred or more nationalities, but the hundred or more nationalities are separately located in different areas of the Soviet Union. We are the most multigroup people and it seems to me that we are becoming, if we do not watch out, the most antigroup people, thereby contradicting all we stand for, and it is against that that this series of addresses is directed.

VI

THE ECONOMIC ISSUE

BY

ELI GINZBERG

Professor MacIver stated in his introductory remarks that I would deal with one phase of the problem of conflict, of how economic struggles were interfering with unity. Frankly, I am not convinced that it is correct to associate, as we all seem to do, *economics* and *conflict*. However, I think it worth while to trace the history of this association. It has something to do, I believe, with one of my collateral ancestors, Karl Marx, not a very close relation but still related. When I chided my father for keeping the relationship hidden he replied that he did not believe in mentioning the black sheep of the family.

There can be no doubt that it was Marx who popularized, in the middle of the nineteenth century, the concept of the class struggle—that great oversimplification of history, poetic perhaps, but still a greatly oversimplified theory that all social experience was explicable in terms of economic conflict between the "haves" and the "have nots."

I know, or better perhaps, I knew Europe from Norway to Sicily. During the past decade, I have traveled widely through these United States. On the basis of what I have seen, I question whether Marx's theory has validity even for Europe. It surely does not fit this country. It is well-nigh impossible to divide this country in two. Geographically and spiritually, we must begin by recognizing at least three regions: The East and Midwest; the South; the Far West. We are as urban as New York City and as rural as northern Minnesota. We know big business in the form of the American Bell Telephone Company, and we have hourly proof of the survival of the corner

77

storekeeper. We have disciplined labor unions, and we have large sections of the country in which a union official is as uncommon as a German prisoner at large. We have large industries which depend primarily upon exports, and we have equally large industries which can scarcely survive without imports. This multiplicity of groups in our body economic does not preclude, however, sharp splits. On rare occasions, usually when tax legislation is under discussion, differences are sunk and lines are drawn tight: one group favors raising the needed revenue by taxing "the other fellow," and the "other fellow" is adamant that the burden be shifted away from him.

These stray comments on the usual lack of cohesiveness in our economic life have distinct bearing on *The Economic Issue*. To begin with, you must permit me to transform *the* economic issue into at least *three* economic issues. Then I will try a magician's trick and dissolve each of the three issues in turn.

The first issue, better still the first economic problem, is concerned with output, with the productivity of our economic machine. We have a large physical plant in this country and a highly developed technology. We have skilled managers and a skilled laboring force. Many conditions must be fulfilled before this economic machine can produce a maximum number of goods and services. Production is the first problem.

Our second problem relates to the many difficulties we encounter in dividing up what we produce. It is no easy matter to decide how much each individual or group is entitled to, nor are we always agreed that every man should get his desserts. Distribution precipitates a host of problems.

The experiences which we have been through these past years have made us, even the most provincial, aware of the fact that the economic life of our country is intertwined with the economic structures of far-distant lands. We must remember that what transpires in Detroit will affect the Malay Peninsula, and developments in Malaysia can have serious repercussions on the economic life of Detroit. For the purpose of this discussion, we will call the third problem foreign economic relations.

The foregoing list of problems could be enlarged, but an extension can serve no useful purpose. We will deal, therefore, with three problems: production, distribution, and foreign economic relations.

I should like to go back to my doctor's dissertation. I refer to it constantly because I remember it, and, what is more, I remember the *Wealth of Nations* with which it was primarily concerned. There is wisdom and insight on almost every page of the *Wealth of Nations* on as many subjects as there are facets to life. It remains a great mystery how a retired professor living on the north shore of the Firth of Forth some forty miles from Edinburgh saw so much farther and so much deeper than his predecessors or successors.

Primary among the new tenets of Adam Smith was his proposition that maximum production could be achieved if each individual in a society were able to go his own way and exploit his own talents with a minimum of interference from government. Smith's appraisal of the civil servants in London would make the most rabid attacks on the New Deal pale in comparison. It was Smith's firm conviction that each individual could figure out his own true interest much better than the bureaucracy could figure out the interests of the country.

The *Wealth of Nations* was published in the same year that witnessed the outbreak of our Revolutionary War. Much has happened on both sides of the Atlantic between 1776 and today. We must therefore check Smith's theory against present-day facts. Let us skip most of the intervening period and concentrate on our experiences since World War I. As you recall, the prosperous twenties were followed by years of depression—1931 was worse than 1930, and 1932 was still worse than 1931. Production sank from one low level to even lower levels, yet the country continued to adhere to the tenets of Adam Smith and shied clear from government interference. There are many brickbats that can be thrown at the Republican administrations of Harding, Coolidge, and Hoover, but it would be unfair to charge them with attempting to run the country from Washington.

We had seven fat years before we ran into the lean years. The prosperous nineteen-twenties should be reviewed if the depression which followed is to be understood. Like a happy marriage, economic prosperity is the result of a successful blending of many strains. First there must be a basis for wide-scale investment, usually in new in-dustries. Investors must be imbued with a belief that profits can be made. And bankers must be willing to share this belief and act upon it. So it was in the twenties. All went well until it collapsed.

Without reviewing the reasons underlying the collapse it is im-portant to recall our behavior during the collapse. As days turned into months, and months into years, we sat and waited, convinced that time would bring its own cure. We waited until one out of every three or four workers was unemployed, until every other machine was out of operation.

Many years have passed since Franklin Delano Roosevelt was first elected Chief Executive. We have probably forgotten the reasons back of the overwhelming vote which he received in 1932. We have probably also forgotten the radical actions which he took in the spring and summer of 1933. The NRA, the FERA, the AAA—the New Deal, in short—was possible because an overwhelming majority voted in favor of a new philosophy in place of the outmoded tenet of "free-dom from government interference." Private business had had its chance, but its funds had failed to flow into new enterprises; in fact, nervous investors turned their assets into cash, bringing the entire country to the brink of chaos. Since private funds had not been forth-coming, there was but one alternative—the state had to step in and invest public moneys.

Most Americans favored government interference, although then, as now, there were disagreements as to details. When next we run into a depression, this country will doubtless be of one mind—that government must act—but disagreements will probably persist con-cerning the extent of the required action or the specific techniques to be employed. In a very real sense, the United States went through a bloodless revolution during the New Deal, and it now appears that the issue of government responsibility for employment is firmly established. Our emergence from the depression of the early nineteen thirties, under the aegis of government, presages that we will act in our own behalf when action next is called for.

Our second problem deals with distribution. In these days of graphs, you are doubtless acquainted with the population-income pyramid: the broad base which accounts for 70 or 80 per cent of the population but only 40 to 50 per cent of the country's income or wealth; the apex with only a few per cent of the population and a sizable amount of the total income. These pyramids highlight the fact that a few people own and control a disproportionate share of the national output.

Current inequalities in distribution do not go unchallenged. Trade unions are constantly working to reduce existing inequalities. By raising wage rates, they seek to enlarge the over-all returns to labor, thereby decreasing the shares of management and ownership.

Labor is not alone in using collective power to influence distribution. During the past decades, agricultural groups have been particularly aggressive. Dissatisfied with the prices of many commodities in the world market, agricultural blocs have sought and obtained government subsidies.

The struggles of labor and agriculture to enhance their shares have been going on for some time, and there is every indication that these struggles will continue in the future. Yet there is more to the problem of distribution. A simple arithmetic example will illustrate the principle that hourly wage rates are seldom the strategic factor in labor's income. If a union succeeds in raising the hourly wage from 50 to 60 cents—a large gain—the worker's annual income will increase approximately $200. If one hitherto unemployed member of the family obtains a job, even at 40 cents an hour, the gain in family income will amount to $800. If the work year is increased from 2,000 to 2,800 hours, the gain in annual income even at a 40-cent hourly wage amounts to $320—against which must be assessed the loss in leisure time. Family income is determined only in part by rates of pay; key to the problem is work and output. There will be considerably more to go around if we keep our economic machine operating at reasonable capacity. If we have a large number of idle men and idle machines, most of us will be poorly off no matter how we distribute what we produce.

One advantage to the constant pulling and hauling about "who gets what" is the large amount of "steam" that society can let off without serious consequences. It is difficult to remember, in the midst of war, the dullness of peace. Contests over distribution are useful social cathartics.

A few words about foreign economic relations, the third problem under discussion. For ease of presentation, I refer again to Adam Smith. Although Smith approved of maximum freedom in domestic trade, he perceived that foreign trade involved considerations of national security which made it necessary to keep a careful check on traders because they had it within their power to precipitate a country into war.

At the conclusion of World War I, we heard much about the role that imperialism played in bringing on hostilities. Students dealing in the origins of that war repeatedly emphasized the friction caused by national groups maneuvering to exploit lucrative areas. Today, imperialism is seldom mentioned. It is the exceptional student who reminds us that our relations to the Japanese are explainable in part by our interest in China; that we could not afford to stand by while Germany made secure her hegemony of all Europe.

The economic interpretation of war is momentarily out of favor. We had best remember, however, that the peace to come will largely depend upon our ability to establish a framework for international economic relations. Anarchism in international economic relations can lead only to war. Mutual commitments translated into formal obligations are the alternative to anarchism. International agreements must, however, be based on faith. One cannot distrust Great Britain and Soviet Russia and, at the same time, co-operate with them. One must be willing to take a position, agree to a set of rules, and then act accordingly. This we have hitherto been unwilling to do. The London Economic Conference of 1933 failed because we decided to attend to our own knitting and turned our back upon a Europe in chaos. We became the victims of our own Yankee shrewdness. Since we must live with other peoples, we had best make an effort to live with them successfully.

To develop a foreign economic policy for the United States (with its heterogeneous economy) is no easy matter, but the fact that it is beset with difficulties is no excuse for avoiding the problem. Automotive manufacturers are interested in low tariffs because they have little to fear in the way of foreign competition here at home. On the other hand, there are many shoe, chemical, and glass manufacturers who remain vitally interested in high tariffs because they are fearful of a rebirth of European trade and export.

Such differences of opinion can be multiplied many times. They illustrate the need of establishing a mechanism for crystallizing American policy on foreign trade. At present, each pressure group works on Congress on its own behalf, which results in a crazy quilt of specific legislation that cannot be dignified with the name "policy." It is essential that we clarify our "national interest," evaluate specific requests in the light of this interest, and encourage the government to take steps to further it. In a world of many nations, we must make commitments, and, to do so intelligently, we must have a policy.

I stated at the outset that I would try to dissolve the three problems of production, distribution, and foreign economic relations. This enterprise takes me into the realm of morals, education, and social philosophy.

What is the relation of morals to production? Simply this: It is amoral to have a physical plant capable of large output and a laboring force desirous of working, and to permit the plant to remain idle and to enforce idleness on the people. The most depressing by-product of a study of "The Unemployed" which I completed several years ago, was the recognition of the widespread lack of interest of the community in the unemployed and the awareness of the unemployed of this attitude. A society which ignores a cancer cannot long survive. It is a moral precept that if goods are required, machines are available to produce them, and workers are pressing for employment, a society must seek a solution even if it cannot achieve one.

Morals are also relevant to discussions concerning distribution. It cannot be a matter of indifference to society that prevailing property relations permit one woman to indulge her taste for esoteric orchids while another must see her child die from lack of medical care. Gross inequalities can be ignored, but only for a time. Either a society remedies or at least mitigates the problem, or else it will be rent asunder by it.

As far as foreign economic relations are concerned, problems of morals are constantly in the foreground. The relations between one people and another are grounded in basic values. If we ignore the treatment which one powerful national metes out to a weaker neighbor, such abrogation of responsibility will sooner or later come back to plague us. Admittedly, no one country, not even the most powerful, can set itself up as the world's policeman. But policing the world must not go by default.

So much for morals. What of education? Let us again use Adam Smith as a point of departure. He realized what has since been forgotten, that the wealth of a nation depends in the first instance on the quality of the people. It is a sad commentary that this insight was lost. If we agree that the wealth of a nation is largely determined by the quality of the people, we can increase wealth by improving quality. As far as Smith was concerned, the differences between a street cleaner and a philosopher were explicable by differences in educational advantages. Despite the large sums which we spend on education, it remains a fact that three out of four of our most talented students are unable to proceed beyond high school because of the economic disenfranchisement of their families. If Smith is right, we are cheating ourselves.

There is still another link between education and the economic issues which we have been reviewing. In a democracy, basic policies are settled at the polls. There is no other place where fundamental issues can be decided. So-called friends of democracy have occasionally contended that fundamental policy questions are so difficult of solution that they cannot be intelligently assessed by the average voter and should therefore be left to the judicious decisions of bureaucrats. Although many issues should not be decided at the polls, basic issues must be decided there. If voters are to rise to the occasion, then policies must be presented in their essence, so as not to obscure and confuse the uninitiated. Further, each voter must possess that minimum of education, training, and discipline that will enable him to choose with discretion.

Where does social philosophy fit into the scheme of things? It is interesting to note in passing that Adam Smith held the chair of moral philosophy at Glasglow. If our twentieth-century sophistication did not make us self-conscious about morals, we would still use the term "moral philosophy." These economic problems which we have reviewed, these issues, these conflicts—at this stage it is no longer important what word we use—can be resolved only by analysis, evaluation, and re-evaluation. That is the work of social philosophy.

The problem of critique is the problem of social or moral philosophy. Until the outbreak of the present war, it was disheartening to witness the repeated unwillingness of the United States to think through its problems either in terms of its past or its future. Without signposts one is lost; initiative is lost. War itself becomes nothing more than a defense reaction.

Social philosophy has much to contribute to considerations of distribution. It alone can assess the reasonableness of techniques to be employed in achieving the ends that are considered desirable. Few favor redistributing wealth by permitting the poor to hold up the wealthy at the point of a gun.

The relation of national advantage to international obligation is definitely a problem in social philosophy. When this war is over, the ten million members of the Armed Forces who return home will not be internationalists. Their experiences in North Africa, Germany, and the Pacific will have made chauvinists of them. They will be disinclined to trade present advantage for future gain. It is the duty of us who remained behind to point out that their sufferings and even more, the sacrifices of those who did not return, were the direct consequence of a breakdown in international relations and, further, that this breakdown reflected an unwillingness on the part of many nations, including our own, to pay the price for order.

One concluding remark: What has economics to do with all this? Simply this: Economics is a way of thinking about how people make a living, and we have seen that in pursuing this problem of making a living, we were forced to deal with the fundamentals of social life—morals, education, and social philosophy. If we have not squared the circle, we have at least closed it.

DISCUSSION

QUESTION: Could you say a little more about protection and free trade?

PROFESSOR GINZBERG: When I do not know the answer, I always go to history because then I cannot be challenged easily. The outstanding trend in the area of protection and free trade appears to be the increasing role played by national governments. During the 1930's, Germany worked out an intricate system of politico-military spheres of interest. She used the profits from this combine to strengthen herself in other areas. Belatedly, but nonetheless surely, Britain replied in kind.

During this war, all trade has been under strict government surveillance. Until the millennium arrives, and national boundaries are eliminated, I think that no state will permit its economic relations with other states to get very far out of control. Apparently, we are moving away from the old simple dichotomy of protection *versus* free trade into the complex arena of the determination of national economic policy by Congress, and government-directed trade under the aegis of the State and War Departments, the consequences of which can scarcely be foreseen, no less evaluated at this time.

QUESTION: Several of us are interested in the proposed legislation considered by this state in the area of discrimination in employment. I wonder if you would discuss this for a moment.

PROFESSOR GINZBERG: This is a moral issue. Our rate of progress will depend upon our success in educating people who now practice discrimination. One can never rise above the source. The majority's negativism toward minority groups is not only emotionally predetermined but also contains a large element of deliberately engendered economic exploitation. It is a problem of leadership to educate the majority to realize that the free expression of emotion and deliberate exploitation will in the larger scheme of things prove harmful not only to the minority but to the majority itself.

QUESTION: In your opinion what gives rise in the minds of servicemen whom you have contacted to a negative feeling toward internationalism?

PROFESSOR GINZBERG: That is an easy question. They have gone through a series of unpleasant experiences: They have been forced to eat poor food; they have slept in unsatisfactory surroundings; they have been unable to converse with the populace. When they have bought trinkets from peoples whom they have freed, they were forced to pay outrageous prices. They have little or no sense of identity with the people whom they have liberated. They have killed and have seen their buddies killed, and they know not to what end.

QUESTION: What hope do we have in postwar situations for any kind of economic boom? If it is going to be a real-estate boom we know where that leads. What else is there?

PROFESSOR GINZBERG: This question really divides in two: Will we have a boom; if we do, of what use can it be, since it will most certainly come to an end? Viewed in terms of our history, we have been a prosperous country, although periods of prosperity have been punctured by economic declines. I have pointed out earlier the important lesson which we learned during the early 1930's, namely, to take action when a decline sets in. As far as the future is concerned, there is no ground for extreme optimism, but there is surely no basis for deep pessimism. The fact that we are now operating our very complex economic machine in a fashion to utilize all our resources is proof that we can manage our economy.

QUESTION: Might it not be said that prior to a depression it was customary for business to build up large surpluses which inevitably resulted in depression? Is there any way out of this dilemma?

PROFESSOR GINZBERG: I am afraid that my old teacher, Professor Mitchell, who has devoted his life to the study of business cycles would find it improper for me to approach the problem of depressions in terms of any single variable such as "surpluses." In general, our knowledge about business cycles has reached the point where we can recognize certain factors which make for trouble and certain other factors which can help to eliminate trouble. Beyond that we are still very much in the dark.

QUESTION: In your opinion, do other nations understand this need for socialization as well as our country does? I do not mean socialism, but socialization in government control. I think of Russia at one extreme and Britain at the other.

PROFESSOR GINZBERG: I feel that on the particular question of socialization we have the most to learn. I am sure that on many other points we have the most to teach.

VII

THE RELIGIOUS ISSUE

BY

RALPH W. SOCKMAN

I think we have to approach these factors of disunity with just one word of leniency. We are cast in a time when events move too fast for our trends of thought to keep up with them. We are not only disunited socially but we are disintegrated, in a way, individually. It is quite understandable why there should be a lag between good intentions and clear convictions, in a world where we think at high tempo and move now in world currents.

But we cannot blame science or technology or modern industry for some of the tensions which divide us. They go back to racial and religious and cultural roots. This brings me down to that most persistent and pernicious thing called prejudice, with which I wish to deal mainly today.

Prejudice has many forms. That blindness of the mind which shutters us against the light of logic and refuses to look facts in the face—that is prejudice. Those little preconceptions which cause the mind to jump to conclusions without looking for causes—those are forms of prejudice. That vampire of suspicion which flies around in the shadows of darkness and sucks the blood of ruddy hopes and good intentions—that is prejudice. That dislike of the different, which makes us attack our pioneers, our prophets, our saints—that is a form of prejudice.

Prejudice is a sin difficult to dislodge because everybody denounces it and no one confesses it. Or if we do confess it, we do it with a shrug, "Oh, yes, I have my prejudices." But we smile them away as if they were a sin that is not very serious. Narrow-minded people do not come clamoring to be saved from their sin of prejudice. If we have prejudices, we do not think we have them, or we laugh them off. And yet these sins of the mind are far more socially destructive than the flagrant sins of the body. One person of high position and privilege with a prejudice can do more harm in society today than a dozen drunken derelicts. We cannot shift this matter of prejudice to the lower strata of society. It must be faced in religious and social circles where opinions are being formed.

What are the sources of prejudice? According to one of its victims, "Prejudice like the spider makes everywhere its home and thrives where there seems nothing to live on." It almost seems as if prejudice has no source; and yet, when we look more deeply, we know it has.

One source is social inheritance. Many of our dislikes are caught in the hazy half-light of childhood, and we never put away those childish things. We have an old saying that we are tattooed with the beliefs of our tribe while we are in the cradle. Some of our prejudices come up out of that infancy, and we have to watch the juncture between the two generations, lest youth get the perverted ideas of their elders. But here is a still more important point: I think the youth of today are one of the hopes in delivering adults from prejudice. Youth are usually far less prejudiced than their elders because prejudice is a learned response. Social inheritance is one source, and it must be watched at the juncture of the two generations.

Another source of prejudice, of course, is ignorance. In a forum down in my church last fall this definition was given: "To have a prejudice is to be down on something you are not up on." I think that pretty well explains where some of our prejudices come from. They come from ignorance. But there again we must not oversimplify the situation and blame only the uneducated group. Here is the sinister fact: The agencies that might have been expected to deliver us from prejudice have not done so. The press which brings us these new horizons has so often been perverted to foment, rather than to dissipate, prejudice. News is often colored. It reflects on certain races and groups and religious bodies. Certain columnists with large followings play upon prejudices.

Also we might expect travel to emancipate us from provincial dislikes. I have been told that many of the young men in the Army and Navy think that after the war we shall popularize travel by cheapening it. This, they believe, will make for better understanding. I wish I could think it was as simple as that. However, in my experiences with travelers I have noted how often travel only serves to pat their preconceptions on the back. A man goes to Paris, for instance, and pays his wife's millinery bill, and then tells you the French are a nation of shopkeepers. Or a man on a Cook's Tour around the world will stop at a Shanghai hotel, talk to a bellboy and return saying that Christian missions are a failure in China. Mere travel is not going to emancipate us.

We might think higher education would free us from prejudice, but education often merely causes people to rationalize their own preconceptions. A great deal of publicity was given to President Shuster's experience at Hunter College last year. May I quote what he said in his message to his faculty: "While every member of the staff is entitled to his or her opinions, indoctrination in terms of these opinions is clearly limited by the rights of parents who send their daughters to us. Such rights cannot in any way circumscribe the process of scholarly or scientific inquiry which is inevitably in part subjective. But it is another thing entirely to undermine the courtesy which underlies our necessary acceptance of cultural pluralism by indulging in quite personal attacks on the convictions, sentiments, and legitimate prides of student groups."

Prejudice and bigotry thrive on ignorance, but in our day of specialization a man may be in the so-called highly educated group, an authority in his own field, and yet be abysmally ignorant in other areas of knowledge. And because he has a certain prestige in his particular field his opinions have undue weight with the crowd. Alfred Noyes has a thesis which I think is quite pertinent, that in our age of specialization we are misled by small clever minds which know their own branches, but have got away from the main stem.

Now, if travel and higher education and the press cannot deliver us from prejudice, we naturally would look to that which we maintain is the main stem of life, religion. But here I have to confess that, as Dr. MacIver said, religious groups have often been divisive. My profound conviction is that the greatest hope of unity in this nation of ours and in the world lies in the area of religious influence. I say this with full knowledge that we have these sectarian and divisive aspects. Nevertheless, our hope lies there. But we have to admit, do we not, in these good-will gatherings of Roman Catholic, Protestant, and Jewish groups, that our people do not know the philosophies of other groups? What is more, we not only read solely the writers of our own groups, but we too often take our impressions of other groups from anonymous and pernicious writers.

The third source of prejudice, which I suppose is still the most important, is fear. It is amazing how deeply rooted in fear are our prejudices. Our dislike of the foreigner is not just because of his difference. You let one foreigner come to a community, and very often he is lionized. I recall that in my college class there was a very likable and gracious young Japanese who was a pet of the campus. But, when they come in larger numbers, we become afraid. Our trade unions become concerned about the standards of living. Our medical profession becomes alarmed about the number of refugee doctors in the community. Our faculty administrators must be alert not to take on too many foreign professors. Numbers, you see, begin to create a fear.

When we get at the root of these religious and racial differences, we find fear rather than real difference of opinion is very often the cause of prejudice. There was really no Roman Catholic issue in the Protestant minds of America until after the Irish and Italian waves of immigration, which made the Roman Catholic church much more dominant in certain sections. Then it became a question not so much of religious differences as of social and political prerogatives. I think we may say that the Jewish question in America came after the tidal immigration that created the element of fear in economic realms. I do not believe that we distinguish sufficiently between economic fear and religious differences. When we get down to it we have to admit that our differences as religious groups root largely in the soil of economic fear and social prestige.

Here is the interesting thing, as Herbert Agar pointed out in his *Time for Greatness.* We Americans are a plot-haunted people, and the rather inconsistent but sinister fact is that those who ought to be the most secure are the ones who are the most fearful; that is, the more possessions we get, the more we make our possessions a part of our personality. This gives us more coastline to defend; the wealthier we are, the larger the coastline. We are not actually in fear of not having the necessities of life. It is wealth for power rather than for use that we crave. As we say, "we want to keep in the swim," which does not mean that we are actually afraid of drowning, but that we want to look well on the beach. We want position and prestige. And then the situation is made worse by the propagandists who capitalize on the fears of people. We cannot keep people from telling lies, but we can take some of the profits out of the propagandists and columnists who play up the fears of the people.

Ours is a sinister situation. The war has done something to unite us. It has done to us something like what danger does to the passengers on a ship. In a normal voyage the passengers on a ship travel in classes, first, second, and third. But if the ship strikes an iceberg or a rock, they know that they are all in the same boat. We have at least learned in the war that we are all in the same boat. But if all that keeps us together is the fear of a foreign foe, then beware of what may happen when the war is over.

If racial or religious prejudices should synchronize with economic depression, and we start looking for scapegoats, then we might have tensions to rival those horrible memories of the Ku Klux Klan.

Having turned our thoughts to the cause of prejudice, let us look now to the more constructive side. In the talk about religious and cultural brotherhood we have reached this stage: We are emphasizing and discussing problems, but we need to make the transfer from the problems of brotherhood to the experiences of fellowship. That is our point of transition. For this we shall need to cultivate humilities.

The first one which I suggest is humility of mind. We need not argue here the reason why pride is the first of the seven deadly sins. It is because it is so poisonous, and, like prejudice, so baffling.

Pride of race is the last vantage point of a small man. When he has nothing else to boast of, he falls back upon race. You know what Professor Franz Boas said: "If we were to select the most intelligent, imaginative, energetic, and emotionally stable third of mankind, all races would be represented."

We ought not to have to argue with intelligent groups any more about racial superiority or inferiority. That is a myth which has been exploded. But we must have humility enough on the part of major groups to recognize it.

Then there is the pride of social position that separates us. We Americans boast that we have no rigid caste distinctions. But we have something in this country almost worse—the cult of success. A man makes his way up the ladder and he says, "If I can do it, the other fellow can, too." The most intolerant on that point are the ones who have just got over the line.

Then comes the pride of opinion. One of the noblest activities of the mind is to sit down in groups like this and exchange our views. But how often discussion deteriorates into mere argument in which the contestants are not trying to find out what is right, but to show just how right they are. Our exchange of opinion is not seeking truth in love. It is so often just sheer argument.

To this pride of opinion must be added the pride of our religious groups. I do not know that I much favor any more the word "tolerance." Tolerance has in it so often a kind of condescension. Good will will never successfully move from one religious or cultural group to another when it moves like a stream from higher to lower level. It must move as the tide moves across the ocean on a level drawn by the attraction of a power above.

We must be humble enough in mind to recognize that truth is so vast that none of us has a monopoly on it. The avenues to it are so broad and so numerous that no group knows them all. We need the modesty of the seeker, the kind of attitude that Huxley had when he wrote to Charles Kingsley and said: "Science seems to me to teach in the highest and strongest manner the great truth which is embodied in the Christian doctrine of entire surrender to the will of God. Sit down before fact as a little child. Be prepared to give up every preconceived notion. Follow humbly wherever and to whatever abyss nature leads or you will learn nothing."

Such humility of mind is far from us. In order to cultivate it, we must start at home. It was said of St. Francis of Assisi that, whenever he had a tendency to become too proud of himself, he got a fellow monk to sit down with him and tell him his faults. Of course, if St. Francis had been married, he would have got that service at home. Home is the place where we should get the elemental attitudes of humility. But what happens at home? Our godly forbears and our ancestors were wont to begin and end the day with a devotional reading. They sat there alone in the presence of God and their sins and their blessings were held up to His light. How do we begin and end our day? With a news broadcast in the morning before breakfast and the last news broadcast at night. Both of them do what? They do not make us humble in the presence of the good God, but rather they make us feel how bad the other people of the earth are. Humility must be taught through the home, the school, and, most of all, through the church, where we sit down to contemplate the vastness of God's truth and the greatness of His power.

I had a rather vivid reminder of it down in Mexico during the summer of 1943. I was taken out to see the new volcano. Five months before, the eruption had begun, and by the time I arrived it was a mountain 2,000 feet high throwing up rocks the size of a piano 2,000 feet higher. At night it was a cone of fire from top to bottom. I think that next to the Grand Canyon it was the most impressive sight which I have ever seen. As we were being driven out to it, the driver discovered on the seat of his automobile a Roman Catholic priest and a Protestant minister. He turned around and said, "You men tell us to be good, but this volcano makes us want to be good." When I got there I saw the point. He looked at that volcano as a revelation of what man might expect as a retribution for his sins. It did not impress me quite that way, but it did impress me with the words of the Forty-sixth Psalm: "The heathen raged; the kingdoms were moved; He uttered His voice, the earth melted." "Be still, and know that I am God." Humility of mind is needed to dissolve these prides of opinion and class and race.

The second attitude for the cure of prejudice is a hospitality of mind. It takes something more than a merely open mind to get what we want in the way of united brotherhood today. Too many open minds are like my sleeping room: in the morning the windows are open and the air too cold to get up in with zest. A lot of minds which we call open are too cold to get up in. They do not stir up any fervor. We cannot have real tolerance unless we have real conviction. Mere openness of mind, mere emptiness of mind, is no ground for a tolerance that will be constructive. For this reason I sometimes, as I say, dislike the word "tolerance."

Professor Lindeman has thrown out an idea which I shall pass on to you: "It seems to me that modern religious institutions—and this applies particularly to those religions which stem from Hebraic-Christian sources—will discover a genuine and redeeming function in this world of tensions, if in the first place they will clearly define the relations of dogma to human welfare. I do not ask the abandonment of dogma, since such a request would ignore realities. I only ask that the part that dogma must play in the preservation and enrichment of human values should be understood and clearly stated."

We cannot throw away dogma. Dogma to us is like the findings of science in the laboratory. But the findings of science do not keep the true scientist from having an open mind toward new values, new discoveries, new explorations. Study our dogmas, but with openness of mind, charity of heart, and humility of spirit.

And lastly, if we are to overcome prejudice we must have an aggressive propaganda for brotherhood. Propaganda, you know, feeds largely on fear and hatred and anger. *The New York Times* pointed that out some year or two ago when it said that to have effective propaganda we seem to need someone to be against. President Lowell of Harvard struck the same note in 1929, when he welcomed to his campus the first of those conferences that have become almost a tradition with us, the National Conference of Christians and Jews.

President Lowell said that this matter of good will resolves itself into the simple question: "Can we generate loyalty and devotion to our own group without playing up hatred and fear of some other group?" The tribe secured its tribal loyalty through fear of other tribes. Parties did the same thing in government. Lowell cited a case in the history of the French Republic when Jules Simon was very much disturbed about the disintegrating of the Republican Party— I am speaking now of the Republican Party in France and not in the United States! Jules Simon was discussing the situation in France. A man in his office said, "Oh, there is always one way we can bring our group together, and that is to take a big crack at the clericals." Simon replied, "The only place for you is out the door."

If we can get loyalty to our group only through fear and hatred and rivalry of some other group, then this vicious circle of wars without and tensions within will go on. We must find some way of generating loyalty by a propaganda *for* things rather than *against* things.

Can we do it? There again we must start with the home. Just think what the home can become as a laboratory of brotherhood if we use our radio broadcasts. At our family tables we can interpret to our children these world outlooks. The school can be another laboratory. Perhaps you know about what is now called the Springfield Plan. About 1939, in that typical American city they set out to generate good will. The educators realized that all the talk about good will was not very realistic. When a Negro girl wanted to get a job, she found that she was handicapped. When a boy with a foreign name wanted to get a position, he found it was not the same as if he had a good old Anglo-Saxon name. Then the Springfield Plan was worked out. The steps were these: Getting axioms of decency and fair play into the minds of the children; emphasizing the difference between facts and opinions; stressing the importance of getting relevant facts in a situation before making a judgment, and with these facts in mind making judgments in terms of decency, honesty, and fair play.

And now we come to the most essential laboratory of good will— religion itself. What we need more even than increased information is a more sensitized imagination. I remember speaking at a good-will round table of Jews, Roman Catholics, and Protestants some years ago. After it was over a woman came up to me and said, "Why do you talk about it so much? It is all so simple. Just practice the Golden Rule: 'Do unto another as ye would that he should do unto you.'" I said, "Yes, that is all there is to it, but the trouble is that most of us haven't enough imagination to know what we would want done to us if we were in the other person's place, with the result that we do to him what we think is good for him, and that usually irritates him."

Archbishop Temple lately passed away, to our great loss. Before his death he said, "This world can be saved from political chaos by one thing only, and that is worship." That sounds like a pious pulpit statement at first, but listen to the definition of "worship": "To worship is to quicken the conscience by the holiness of God; to feed the mind with the truth of God; to purge the imagination by the beauty of God; to open the heart to the love of God; to devote the will to the purpose of God."

If worship meant to us that; and if when we come into our houses of worship and pray to God, the Father of all men, we were to feel ourselves in a room with a mirror in the ceiling and looking up into the mirror, we should thus be enabled to look down better into the other person's place, then we would be getting that sensitized imagination necessary to make good will work.

Robert Frost tells of a New England farmer who was patching up his stone fence which the winter weather had disintegrated. As he was laying the stones up he said, "Something there is that doesn't love a wall." That something is God.

DISCUSSION

QUESTION: Dr. Sockman, a teacher of my acquaintance feels that in the classroom he must, so far as possible, keep from any kind of expression of personal opinion, personal prejudice, on however high a plane it is. I mean prejudice against prejudice, for example. But he feels that when he is asked directly by a student, privately, for his opinion on any subject he is not only free to but should reply. The same question might be asked of a minister. What do you think of that?

DR. SOCKMAN: I think any teaching, as Dr. Shuster said, is bound to be partly subjective. We cannot be purely objective. I think we certainly have to give the impression of honesty and sincerity when we try to answer. I think there is a little difference in taking the initiative in making statements and answering a direct question put to you. I should say that if a pupil raised a question, you must give that pupil an honest answer. It might be something that you yourself would not put up on the horizon of his thought. We can, however, be good teachers only if we are honest and try to convey our own convictions. So I should think a teacher would be bound to answer a question, even a question that might be interpreted as a matter of religious belief, in sincerity and honesty.

QUESTION: There is the element of indoctrination.

DR. SOCKMAN: That is a very difficult question. I should be very glad to have some of you teachers discuss it. Of course, that is what we ministers live on, indoctrination. It is one thing in the church where they come of their own free will and another thing in the public school. However, I do not quite see how you can get away from what might be charged as indoctrination.

We keep repeating the old formula that it is our business to teach people how to think and not what to think. But open-mindedness is not like a kit of plumber's tools that you can carry around and put down any place. You learn open-mindedness in concrete situations. We have to take everything in its own concrete setting. It seems to me that, if we are going to teach people how to think, we are bound to give them some content of what to think, indirectly or through our own teachings.

QUESTION: Dr. Sockman, we live in an atmosphere of vicious propaganda to a great extent. You say counterpropaganda so often arouses the suppressed groups, arouses their antagonism sometimes. Perhaps the method for meeting vicious propaganda is the Springfield Plan for churches or religious groups. What is the best sort of Springfield Plan for religious groups that you have in mind?

DR. SOCKMAN: I should say that we ought to be giving our own groups better information regarding other groups, not just having them take what they get from anonymous and often pernicious sources.

I should say that we should get our young people to hear distinguished leaders of other faiths and communities. Too often in getting together with these good-will groups, we just say the nice little amenities; we never enter into any discussion of our beliefs. This will not get us very far, of course. We really need to know more about what the Protestant, Catholic, and Jewish faiths teach.

My feeling is that if Springfield could do it in an American city—they had all the cross currents and all the different colors and complexioned groups—our churches ought to be able to do it.

I like to think that we are making progress in that willingness to listen. Do you think we are? I can only speak for my own church. In fact, we have a forum each fall. We had one or two rabbis speak, and we had Dr. Shuster of Hunter College, a distinguished Roman Catholic. I do not know that a Roman Catholic priest would come to a Protestant church to speak, but we have had Roman Catholic priests for certain occasions. I am willing to go as far as I can.

QUESTION: I don't think the schools have any moral-education programs at all. Springfield has, but the schools are not giving moral education, are they?

DR. SOCKMAN: Except for very infrequent occasions, I should say.

QUESTION: They have no extensive and intensive educational program in the churches, and the schools really do not have sufficient time or give sufficient time to that. We are not doing much about it, either, are we?

DR. SOCKMAN: No, certainly not in New York. But in some places it is done, you know. I presume we do not parallel that in our situation. But this separation of church and state has led to what was referred to as a complete nullification of moral teaching. In my opinion that is a very deplorable situation. If religion is the source of culture, if it is that main stem through which life comes out in all these other branches and we shut it off from our youth, the result is bound to be ultimately, I think, deleterious, if not completely devastating.

QUESTION: Do you want to give it to them? Don't you want to set the stage so that these people working would have it and take it in by absorption? I mean, you just can't set up a moral program to give to somebody. All the people working in it have to have this spirit of humility and all those things.

DR. SOCKMAN: I quite agree with you.

QUESTION: It has to start with us first. We have to change ourselves and then hope to have that carry over to change others.

DR. SOCKMAN: Nevertheless, there are certain great ethical traditions, ethical lines of teaching, that I am not sure a youth would catch just by indirect influence. You have to know something about whence we get our secret of strength. Of course, I do think this: we try to do by agitation what we fail to do by demonstration. That is, the moment we want to try to correct any abuse we seek to try to cure it by agitation. Let the light shine and somebody will see it. But somebody has to put the light on the candlestick, that is the point.

Here, for example, the Negro, I think, will have to admit that he has got to demonstrate the virtues which he claims. But nevertheless somebody must help the Negro race to get up on the candlestick where the light can shine. I think it will take a certain amount of—I will call it active propaganda.

QUESTION: I think we agree with you when you state that in sitting down to be open-minded we often sit down with a tendency to sort of defend ourselves, to show how right we are, rather than see who is right. That would follow in with what somebody else has just said.

But in my mind there is the fact that something has to be done, don't you think, with some of our textbooks? There is too much propaganda in some of them, especially in reference to history books. Don't you think so?

DR. SOCKMAN: Now you are going into a field that I did take a degree in once, history. That is your field also, Professor MacIver, and you are more conversant with the textbooks than I am. Have you something specific that you would like to give us? I have read reports but I don't know.

QUESTION: I was thinking not only of the textbooks, but what you mentioned before, the press. I picked up the *Times* this morning and read an article in it. I think Mr. Wallace made the statement that we had been misinformed about Russia. I don't know how far some of us agree, or whether I agree myself, but the fact remains that in history books—especially United States history books—the distortion of the facts of the Civil War period, say, or the Reconstruction period, or the distortion of the facts that center around or hinge around our wars with other countries, sort of breeds in us hatred, say, against the United Kingdom, or Spain, or any of the countries.

DR. SOCKMAN: I quite agree with your position that we should sift as far as we can the colored information that tends to make a perversion of thought. I am assuming that that is being rather progressively done. I don't know. I hear agitation about it. It certainly is a point.

QUESTION: I take it that people will reject the help of the churches in this communication and fellowship and brotherhood, because they say the churches are not united, the religious groups are not united, and they have no right to ask others to do what they cannot do themselves. What are you going to say to those people? What will you do about it?

DR. SOCKMAN: You have a very good point against us. I know that. A disunited church is a weak voice calling for a united world. That is certainly very true. As a Protestant I admit the tragedy of the 256 Protestant groups in this country—it is something like that number, I believe. However, those critics may magnify some things. I find that churches can work together on some of these questions without organic unity. As long as we have differences of temper, differences of approaches to God, I think we are bound to have differences of religious organization.

However, it seems to me that with consecration and devotion we should strive to have a united voice in these questions. We are not pleading for a world with just one political setup. We are pleading for a world that respects the different types of government in the different countries. We are not going to try to make a democracy out of Russia. I think we have an attitude now that is better than the one in the past war. We are not striving for that now. I think the church should have that, even though it is not the same organic union.

QUESTION: Do you believe the church is responsible for the prejudices we have?

DR. SOCKMAN: I think the church is one of the factors in social inheritance and in ignorance and in keeping people uninformed. The church is involved in all I have mentioned. I would not say it was the chief factor; I do not know. I want to be humble and say that I recognize the divisiveness and sectarianism and narrowness in all religious forces. I recognize that. On the other hand, I still assert that if we are humble enough to recognize that, we have that atmosphere-creating body that is necessary today. I would not go quite so far as to say that we are the chief cause of this, but we are one, and let us be humble and mention it.

QUESTION: Those words you mentioned of Archbishop Temple's are, in my opinion, a wonderful blueprint for religion, and one which a young mind could really take in. How can we get that aspect of religion across to the growing generation, to children, some of whom are born atheists, and sometimes atheists of two generations, and many times of homes of artificial or sectarian beliefs? They cannot believe it because it is not suited to their minds. How can we get that kind of religion to these children, our children?

DR. SOCKMAN: We can do that only by what was said here a while ago, I think, by the influence of those who have it first. We recognize that that interpretation by Archbishop Temple is not the prevailing interpretation of religion as it is given in the pulpits of the country. It would seem to me that that definition he gives could be put into almost any school, to have a period where they can get that conception without any indoctrination that would be offensive. Indoctrination of religion, yes, but only atheists could object to that. But it will have to start with the church, with religious groups, and grow and spread as we get more catholicity of mind, more imagination. There is no short cut to spreading that kind of view. It simply must be the multiplication of the cell principle spreading through our whole body politic.

QUESTION: I would like to ask what you meant when you said the Negro would have to demonstrate more his position? I think we have demonstrated it from our two hundred years in this country.

DR. SOCKMAN: Yes, and I agree with you there thoroughly. The point is, I think we have to convince people by what we do. As we go along, agitating at the same time, other groups, majority groups, must help those who do not get a fair chance to show what they can do. I quite agree with the speaker that the Negro does show that, but the public does not always know it. We must help that light to be up on a candlestick where they can see it. I think there are some signs that we are making progress along that line, although we know how tragically slow is the recognition of the Negroes' achievements.

I do not want to give the impression at all that I thought the Negro had not demonstrated his position. I simply wanted to get the impression out that we convince by demonstration rather than by agitation alone. That applies to all. I merely used that as an illustration. That applies to all groups, including my own, of course.

PROFESSOR MACIVER: One of the best signs of the success of these meetings is that they are getting harder and harder to bring to an end. I must say one word, however, because I have been appealed to with regard to this matter of indoctrination.

No teacher should regard his job as indoctrination. But when he is teaching his subject he cannot help in some way doing a bit of indoctrination. It all depends on what the subject is. If you are teaching the elements of geometry you should not go out of your way to say what you think of Mohammedans, or comment on the Democratic Party or the Republican Party. That is irrelevant. All irrelevant indoctrination should at once be ruled out. What you cannot rule out is the presentation of your conclusions regarding relevant matters concerning which there is evidence on both sides. I do not agree with those who say, "Well, let us state things and not draw any conclusions."

My field is political, or social, science. What I try to do, or hope to do, is to give all the evidence as favorably to one position as to the other; not to omit, not to distort. The real danger of indoctrination is distortion.

It is not setting forth what is known. It is the deliberate or even the unconscious presentation of one part of the truth or one part of the evidence. If you do not do this, you must be entitled to give your conclusions.

PART THREE

WHAT WE CAN DO ABOUT THEM

VIII

WHAT THE SCHOOLS CAN DO [1]

BY

CLYDE R. MILLER

In any society, the schools mirror the forces which control that society. So when we ask, What can the schools do in a situation which is filled with danger? we must also ask, What can representatives of the groups which really run American communities do? The schools can do little alone.

You have heard here four or five presentations which might be likened to diagnoses: What is wrong with this world? We come today to the first of a series of prognoses. What are we going to do about it?

It may be worth while to attempt to picture the task which is before American communities, including, of course, the schools. Nowhere has that picture been brought to me so vividly as by an item cabled to America July 3rd or 4th, 1944, by the American newspaper correspondent, J. Edgar Murray.

[1] Since this lecture was delivered there have been published three books which describe aspects of the Springfield Plan, a type of community-wide education to prevent prejudice: *The Story of the Springfield Plan* by Alice Halligan and Clarence Chatto, published by Barnes and Noble; *The Springfield Plan—A Photographic Record* by Alexander Alland and James Waterman Wise, published by Viking Press; *The Process of Persuasion* by Clyde R. Miller, published by Crown Publishers. *The Process of Persuasion* develops in detail some of the points made in this lecture, particularly those involved in conditioned reflexes and immunization against dangerous propaganda. Also available are two descriptions of the Springfield Plan which may be obtained in pamphlet form from the League for Fair Play, 11 West 42nd Street, New York 18, N.Y.: "How Your Town Can Build Real Democracy," a reprint of a series of articles on the Springfield Plan which appeared originally in the Bridgeport, Conn. *Sunday Herald;* "The Springfield Plan for Education Against Intolerance and Prejudice," by Dr. Benjamin Fine, Education Editor of *The New York Times,* a reprint of an article which appeared in *The Menorah Journal.*

Mr. Murray told about being on a bus, presumably in London, and suddenly one of those robot bombs appeared headed straight for the bus. It was coming at house-top level, in a slanting dive, and it seemed certain that the bus would be hit. Somebody yelled a warning and everybody fell on the floor, while the driver did what was obviously necessary. He went full speed ahead to get from under the thing. Here Murray told about lying on the floor, when all at once the bus came to a sudden stop; then with a grinding of gears, the bus jerked forward full speed. Then a thunderous crash. The thing had hit. It certainly jarred the people on the bus, but nobody was hurt. The passengers surveyed the damage and were ready to go on again, but the driver, a bit proud of himself for having saved these people from what would have been certain death or terrible injury, couldn't help saying to them: "Did you see how I dodged that one? I pulled right out from under that cookie. I couldn't get the clutch in for a minute and I thought we were all goners, but I pulled away just in time. I was looking the bloomin' thing right in the face when it blew up."

It occurred to Mr. Murray that the passengers' margin of safety would have been greater if the bus had not stopped. So he asked the driver, "But why did you stop the bus back there?"

"Oh," said the driver, "I couldn't help it. The traffic light went red." And then added this sentence, which is significant: "Then I got hold of myself and drove right through it."

The robot bombs coming at us as the war ends are large-scale unemployment, group bitterness, and violence. Will the stoplights in the form of old habits, conditioning, automatically abort our attempts to deal with these evils? Or will we get hold of ourselves, in time? Here we face a problem in public health—mental health. We must deal with conditioned minds, minds receptive to highly dangerous persuasions which, thanks to our amazingly efficient channels of communication, come at us with such endless repetition as virtually to give us—as Elsa Maxwell of *The New York Post* said in her column yesterday—something like mass hypnotism.

We read about this sort of thing in Lynn Thorndike's accounts of mass manias in the Middle Ages. We can read about it in the classic volumes of Andrew Dickson White, *A History of the Warfare of Science with Theology*. Sumner in his *Folkways* gives many examples of these manias and phobias. Influenced by them, whole populations can be swept off their feet and carried over the abyss to catastrophe. Mass literacy and speed of communication make mass phobias peculiarly dangerous today. In modern Germany, with the most effective school system in the world, the highest rate of literacy in Europe, with universities of glorious tradition of learning in science and scholarship, we have seen these mass phobias at their worst.

Go to the Orient. If Germany had the highest literacy rate in the West, Japan had it in the East. Indeed, it is said that Japan has achieved the highest literacy rate of any nation; yet the people of Japan developed mass phobias too. Mass literacy, efficient schooling, simply made the process easier. Germans and Japanese were conditioned to respond automatically, as those who controlled the schools wished—as that London bus driver responded to the traffic light, as Pavlov's dog responded to the ringing of a bell. Our own task in America is to recondition the minds of millions, to immunize these millions against the contagious phobias which grow out of insecurity, group hatred, and scapegoatism.

Leo Cherne, in his book *The Rest of Your Life,* makes predictions which, to anyone who is familiar with group tensions, are appallingly reasonable. He sees, for the rest of our lives, these tensions increasing. He sees the resulting bitterness taking root. He sees new disorders, of which we had a foretaste in war, disfiguring the American scene.

I was in Cincinnati on D-Day, when nine thousand white workers of Wright Aeronautical walked out. Why? Did they want more money? No. Seven Negroes were moved up from menial jobs to mechanic's jobs.

Can you blame the white workers, though, when the Red Cross and the Navy and the Marine Corps and the Army also say, "We are superior, we white people; we cannot mix our superior selves with inferior groups"?

We Americans are human, too, as are the Germans and the Japanese. We, too, respond to conditioning. We are like our enemies. Like the Germans and Japanese, though not to the same intensity and extent, we, too, have been conditioned to act in accord with the dangerous delusions associated with today's mass phobias.

These "signal words" like Jew, Catholic, Negro, Communist, New Deal, government planning, Wall Street, labor union, are the stimuli to keep us stalled when we ought to be going ahead fast to escape the destruction which is heading for us.

Let us look at these delusions. The first is the delusion that one's own church, cult, sect, or group has all the answers, that only it represents God's will on earth, and that only what it tells people reveals God's purposes.

We observe the perfect flowering of this delusion in Shintoism in Japan, in Emperor worship. The Emperor is God. Treason against the nation is also blasphemy against God. But this delusion is not confined to Japan.

The second delusion is that one race is superior. The Japanese and Germans suffer badly from that delusion, too. So do millions of Americans.

The third delusion is the notion that one class is superior, and therefore should push other people around. When these three delusions are blended together, they reinforce one another. Thus we see God's sanction expressed through the one true church, justifying what the superior race does at the command of its elite.

These three delusions are age-old.

There is a fourth, also age-old—the delusion that there are not enough goods to go around in this world; there are not enough jobs to go around. This is the delusion of scarcity. It was not a delusion up until the beginning, shall we say, of this century. What our scientists have been able to accomplish through mass production has made possible the end of the age of scarcity.

We now live in an age of abundance—at least potential abundance. Nonetheless, we are all conditioned to the age of scarcity. Many of our financial and economic arrangements and labor arrangements (particularly in the A.F. of L.) are based on the delusion of scarcity. It is as though people said: "There are not enough goods to go around, and not enough jobs. Our group is superior. We'll grab off for our group, therefore, what goods and what jobs there are."

Such talk and actions strengthen group antagonisms.

What can the schools do about this? They cannot do much until and unless the citizens who control schools want the schools to tackle the problem.

To begin with, it is necessary that some citizens know these delusions for what they are and how their persistence can make Mr. Cherne's prophecies come true. If there is vast unemployment after this war, we shall witness a terrifying increase in group antagonisms. We shall see our resources in manpower destroyed in these antagonisms. We shall see our physical resources, which might be building a higher standard of living, not being utilized. It will be a disgraceful spectacle.

We can get in a bitter state of mind when we contemplate the stupidity, ignorance, and greed which keep the four dangerous delusions alive. But bitterness will do no good. It is as silly to be bitter about a businessman, religionist, labor leader, Negro hater, anti-Semite, afflicted with these delusions, as it would be for a doctor to be bitter about a person afflicted with tuberculosis or typhoid. Adult citizens who control school policy need something of the physician's detachment before they can be expected to encourage school administrators and teachers to take measures to immunize pupils against phobias associated with unemployment, racial and religious antagonisms. We need to step out of our characters, so to speak, to know our own conditioning. We are helped in this by understanding the conditioning of others. For example, I was brought up in a strong anti-Catholic community, and I was terribly afraid of Catholics. When I reached high school I had close association with Catholic youngsters and came to think they were as good as the best of us. I was speaking of that experience to a New York friend. He said: "You should have known my grandfather. The old gentleman was a Scotch Presbyterian who lived near Boston. We boys lived with him. He had three convictions: No. 1, there is no earthly good in a Democrat. No. 2, the demon rum is the source of all evil. And No. 3, the Roman Catholic Church is the summation of all evil. And he did not like the Catholics any better when they built a church next to the house and shut the light out of the living room.

"It was the habit of grandfather to have a sort of supper-table discussion of the affairs of the day. We got ammunition for that discussion from the Boston paper that came up on the late afternoon train. One day the paper carried a story of a Boston Presbyterian church burning down, with a two- or three-column cut of this flaming edifice on page 1. Somewhere the reporter had written, 'The cause of the fire is unknown.' Of course, that came up for discussion. One of the boys at the supper-table remarked 'They don't know what set that church on fire.'

"I can see grandfather yet, tapping on the table: 'You mark my words, when they find out who set that fire, they'll find it was a low, sneaking, Democratic, rum-drinking Catholic!'"

That incident is far enough removed from today's tension to give us perspective and detachment. Moreover, all of us can laugh at the old gentleman's bitterness. We need that detachment, and the fellowship which comes through laughing together, to approach today's and tomorrow's tensions with reasonable hope of averting the disasters they threaten. We need to know why people think and act as they do. To immunize children and adults against the dangerous delusions, we must have, with detachment, humane ideals. We must face the problems presented by these delusions as scientifically as the competent physician faces the problem of physical and mental disease. Humane ideals alone are not enough. Let me illustrate.

In the *World Telegram* for November 17, 1941, appeared an article which quoted Dr. Hartill, Assistant Superintendent of Schools in Harlem, as saying that the schools do too good a job in the New York community; they unfit the pupils for outside. Let me give directly the words of Dr. Hartill as quoted by the *World Telegram:*

At school we give them the kind of life that exemplifies the best theories of the American way of life.

At 3 o'clock they go out into a different world, with other theories of life. They are thrown in contact with whites who have not made up their minds to accept them as Americans. They have no place to play, literally no home to go to, for their mothers often are working on Park Avenue until 9 o'clock at night.

We break our necks to find what the kids are fitted for. If they show aptitudes for airplanes or auto mechanics, we capitalize on those interests.

Then, when we send them to vocational high school, they're told, "Look here, son, it's no use your trying this. The industry won't let you in." They're frozen out of the aviation industry and many other industries —with no credit to the unions—and they're barred from the profession.

The trouble is, the Board of Education's policy is too far in advance of what the average white wants. So we feed the children on dreams, teach them what the world ought to be.

And the boys come back and say, "This ain't so, mister."

Obviously we shall get nowhere feeding either children or adults on dreams. Those Negro youngsters in Harlem know that the phrase, "liberty and justice for all," simply does not hold for Negroes in America.

This brief story about Harlem indicates that our schools, newspapers, churches, business establishments, and some labor unions have contributed to a training of children and adults to entrench deeply in their minds and hearts the delusion that one race is superior. The first step educational leaders must take in dealing with these four delusions is to recognize that they exist and are widely accepted. The humblest teacher or the most obscure administrator who recognizes it, and acts on it, can become an educational leader. Such teachers and administrators are in a minority. These delusions are folkways. They comprise our climate of opinion. People who denounce them may be called anything from "Nigger lovers" to "Communists." In a community where such delusions are generally held, it would be impossible for the schools alone to do much more than preach the safe futilities of sweetness and light.

However, the task of facing the reality of getting these delusions out of people's heads and hearts must be done. Moreover, it can be done. Good beginnings have been made in many cities: Pittsburgh, Newark, Columbus, Detroit, Springfield. To be successful the task must begin and continue as a community project. It need not start with the schools. A businessman, a minister, a newspaper writer, a P.T.A. member, any man or woman of good will and intelligence and a zeal for building a better community can get under way an education to build the new faith. It goes without saying that such a person will have freed himself from the four dangerous delusions. It also would go without saying that, while recognizing that this task must be started quickly, he also knows that these delusions are folkways. Most people who hold them know not what they do. They cannot be separated from them by violent argument. They can be set free within a few weeks by an approach which I shall give in a moment. First, let me say that in any community a teacher or school administrator or any other person who sees the need of going full speed ahead in creating an education that will prevent unemployment and inequality and their associated delusions should organize a group of adults to get the job done in that community. That is how starts have been made in Springfield, Pittsburgh, Newark, Columbus, and other cities. In Springfield, the school superintendent saw the need to strengthen democracy; in Pittsburgh, it was the wife of a businessman; in Columbus, it was a printer; in Cincinnati, it was a businessman. These persons got others interested. In each community they formed a group to study the local situation. Not everywhere did they see it in clear focus in terms of these four delusions. Most frequently, the impetus has come from a sense of the wastefulness of religious and racial antagonisms. Once a small group organizes within a community, its first task is to educate its own members in what needs to be done in the community and in America. In Springfield (Mass.), where the schools took the initiative but soon had the co-operation of various adult agencies, teachers and other adults were given an opportunity through a series of planned discussions to lay the groundwork for the task to be done.

Let me briefly outline what can be done at five meetings of a group of any community eager to create a partnership of schools with other community agencies—churches, business groups, labor unions—to eliminate the four delusions.

First meeting. Show the contributions of democracy to fair play. Take the word "democracy" out of the class of Rosy Glow glittering generalities. Run it through a prism. Break it into a spectrum of political, economic, social, and religious democracy. These are all inter-related. It is hard to say that one is more important than another unless we agree with Professor Carr that the moral issue associated with Judaism and Christianity is the main issue. Once we accept the ethics of the Prophets and of Jesus, our ideas of racial and class superiority are knocked into a cocked hat. So, too, is our uncharitableness toward those who hold different theological opinions. The emphasis here is on ethics, not on theology. Religious democracy is the right to hold almost any theological opinion so long as holding it does not hurt other people. It involves separation of ecclesiastical organizations from the state.

Religious democracy involves the moral obligation to be decent in human relationships, to play fair.

Political democracy is the right to vote. That implies the right to know the issues on which we vote, the right to talk about them, print pieces in newspapers and handbills about them, and bring them into the schools for discussion. These things are not only rights but obligations. The right to vote means little unless it is accompanied by the right to eat.

Economic democracy is the right to eat. This means the obligation and the right to work, for everybody to have something to say about working conditions and wages. It means the right of employees as well as employers to organize. It involves the obligation of such organizations to co-operate for everybody's welfare.

Social democracy means everybody's welfare. It means that everybody ought to be free from discrimination or persecution based on the delusion of superior race, religion, class, and the delusion of necessary scarcity. From the Prophets of Judaism, from Jesus and the church fathers, from popes, rabbis, and Protestant ministers the ethics inherent in political, economic, social, and religious democracy have been endorsed again and again. Use these endorsements. They can build for acceptance of standards of fair play just as effectively (and to better purposes) as testimonials can sell cigarettes, face creams, and patent medicines.

Second meeting. Show how the new facts of abundance of resources and jobs end the fears which convert prejudice into violence. Simple axioms make the revelation vivid.

(1) Life should be worth living—not only just for the white, or more properly the pink, race but for all races of people for the reason that all are God's children.

(2) In order to live one must have air, water, food, shelter.

(3) There is enough air for everybody, and enough water. Professor Mather, Henry J. Kaiser, Charles Wilson of General Electric, and an increasing number of business executives know that we have the resources to give enough food, clothing, shelter, and all the necessities and some of the luxuries of life to everybody. This is no longer a matter for debate. Our production record and job record in World War II have established it as a demonstrated fact.

(4) This abundance under present economic arrangement has not been utilized, has not been distributed. Note the bulletin of the National City Bank of New York in September, 1942: "The problem is one of organization of production and distribution that all may benefit. This will be the challenge of the postwar economic world."

(5) Habits based on scarcity persist. This is understandable. Scarcity itself persisted until science made available the means to end it. The moral and economic issue is to utilize these means. Until World War II came we did not do that. We destroyed or reduced production of food and textiles. We cut down on production and manufacture of resources because we were conditioned to scarcity economy and profits, which we thought came only through relative scarcity of goods. That meant scarcity of jobs. Fear of being out of work coupled with the false opinions that one's particular race or religion or economic group was superior, brought discrimination against Catholics, Jews, Negroes, foreigners, and others. This applied in the field of jobs. Production in World War II showed what can happen when machinery, resources, and manpower are fully utilized. Even then, old habits based on the delusion of scarcity and on racial, religious, and class superiority made it necessary to set up the Fair Employment Practice Committee in Washington. Such committees are needed in every state along with fair education and fair housing committees.

Third meeting. Show how science, in remaking the physical world, **has** made possible the end of scarcity. Stress how science must **now** tackle the job of human relationships. Show how folkways are made —useful ones as in barn-raisings or traffic regulations; harmful ones such as those based on notions of inferiority and skin pigmentation. Show the difference between fact and opinion; between opinions correctly drawn from relevant facts and those incorrectly drawn. Note the harm that comes when opinions are based on ignorance and superstition, as for example the opinions of a few centuries ago that some persons were witches and should be put to death. Show how the science of anthropology destroys all factual basis for prejudice based on racial difference.

Fourth meeting. Show how persuasions based on false opinion and appealing to long-established habits and fears are spread by word of mouth, newspapers, radio, and other channels of communication. These opinions strongly held become obsessions and phobias. They are contagious. One person can infect others. Given access to the channels of communication, a Hitler, a Coughlin, a Gerald L. K. Smith, a Pegler, a Hearst, or a Martin Dies can infect millions of others. In Germany we see an entire nation obsessed by phobias based on the four great delusions. This meeting should inspire the group to make further study of the devices of persuasion and the mental processes to which they appeal. Understanding propaganda and persuasion is of central significance in the attack on the four delusions.

Fifth meeting. Outline a plan to organize your community for a continuous education to immunize people against the dangerous prejudices and phobias associated with the four delusions.[2]

At this meeting it is essential that responsibility be placed upon a committee of persons eager to achieve co-operation among business groups, labor unions, churches, social agencies, newspapers, radio stations, civic agencies, and schools.

As this committee develops its work, one phase of which should include a survey of group tensions in a community, it can report from time to time its findings and progress to the original group. Within a few weeks the group should be ready to create a permanent

[2] In preparation for this meeting write to the superintendent of schools in Springfield and Pittsburgh for information as to how citizens and school authorities in those cities proceeded in developing community programs to strengthen democracy.

organization linking schools with adult agencies to carry forward continuously an education that will immunize against dangerous phobias by strengthening democracy within the community.

Many teachers and school administrators are alert to the great need which faces most American communities. They can venture no further than adult leadership in the community permits. The imperative responsibility, therefore, in communities all over America rests upon the adults who know how grave our danger is and who are eager to defend us against it by a more humane and scientific education at every school level and in every adult organization.

That the task can be done is clearly demonstrated by the manner in which it is getting under way in various communities. Citizens who become interested in this crucially necessary work will be heartened and encouraged to discover many teachers and school administrators eager to co-operate with them. The main thing that has been holding the schools back has been the lack of encouragement from the people who, in the last analysis, control the schools.

IX

WHAT THE PRESS CAN DO

BY

GERALD W. JOHNSON

In his introduction of me, Doctor MacIver omitted the final qualification that I have to speak on this subject. Whether by politeness or not, I do not know. He mentioned that I am a newspaperman by profession, but he failed to add that I am an escaped newspaperman. Therefore, I am in a position to say the things that all the boys would like to say, but discretion forbids.

I am going to begin with a series of definitions of terms, so simple, so exact, so precise, that they may be absurd. But it is better to be absurd than to be misunderstood, particularly at this time.

Among all the calamities that afflict us today, few are more serious than ambiguous talk, especially about national and international affairs—and the world is full of it. The general subject of the series is "Threats to American Unity" and how to meet them. My particular subject is "What the Press Can Do."

I take up first the word "press" and define it as meaning the daily newspaper press. Press, of course, might include books, pamphlets, magazines, and anything else that comes off the press, or is printed. But to hold the discussion anywhere within reasonable bounds, the line must be drawn somewhere, and I choose to draw it at the daily press. That is the only part that I know anything about.

Journals of opinion, weekly and monthly magazines, broadsides, pamphlets, and books have their problems, but they are very different from those of the daily press.

I wish to comment on the verb as well as the noun. "What the Press Can Do." If "can do" means what the press can do directly,

119

immediately, and consciously toward the elimination of conflict among social groups in this country, the discussion is over now, for the answer is, "Not a thing in the world!"

The reason for this is obvious. The daily-newspaper press is powerless to eliminate conflict among groups directly, because it belongs to a group—that of the industrial corporations. In large cities it belongs to a group of large corporations. A newspaper in a large city represents an investment of millions. It is a manufacturing enterprise, distinguished from others mainly by the fact that it manufactures the most perishable product known to industry. Modern methods of refrigeration will keep ice cream in perfect condition for months. A newspaper spoils within an hour, and nothing short of the interruption of time itself could keep it fresh.

The men in charge of newspaper production are almost always managers, rarely proprietors. Therefore, they are subject to the limitations that lie upon all managerial workers—they are responsible to their stockholders. Sometimes they are hampered and harassed by interference from the owners, from other forces, from advertisers, and what not.

Even when they are free from overt control, they cannot escape their own consciences. They are responsible for millions of dollars of other people's properties. A conscientious man handling other people's money will avoid risks that he would cheerfully accept, were he risking only his own.

Therefore, an aggressive social policy adopting new methods to meet new conditions is no more to be expected of daily newspapers than it is to be expected of national banks, and for the same reason. Both are run by men responsible for other people's money.

This is why the daily newspapers have been so astonishingly ineffective in national politics for the past twelve years. A numerical majority and, measured by circulation, an overwhelming majority of American daily newspapers, opposed Mr. Roosevelt constantly, consistently—many of them, violently, in four successive elections. Four times the people rejected their advice. I do not believe this was because Mr. Roosevelt was the indispensable man or because a majority of the people thought he was indispensable. Mr. Roosevelt was a pathfinder, and he never was opposed by another pathfinder. If Mr. Willkie really belonged to that group, nobody knew it at the time he ran.

There is no denying the fact that pathfinders are frequently dangerous to vested interests. Mr. Roosevelt ruined many vested interests. Perhaps some of them ought to have been ruined—but that is not the point. When new paths are being broken, some vested interests are bound to suffer. Therefore, all are highly nervous. Any going concern is a vested interest, including daily newspapers.

Hence, whenever an aggressive social policy is being aggressively pressed, the daily press must, in the nature of things, view the situation with alarm. If some grow querulous and unreasonable, what else could be expected?

Is the daily press, then, to be dismissed as hopeless? Is it impossible for it to be useful as an agency to reduce social conflicts? The answer must be conditional. If the newspapers choose to cling to the old conception of themselves as the molders and shapers of public opinion, the answer is Yes.

It is not safe for the public to permit newspapers to mold its opinion on the larger social problems because the newspapers are, of necessity, committed to a particularist point of view—the point of view of industrial corporations. There are exceptions, certainly; but this applies to the group. There is no implication of dishonesty in this. In my experience, and it goes for thirty years, the intellectual integrity of individual newspapermen rates as high as that of any group in the population. But they are no more fit to be dictators of public opinion than are the clergy, who also rate high in personal integrity but who are also committed to a point of view.

A newspaperman is not and, in the nature of things, cannot be altogether a free agent. He is the servant of an institution. The more conscientious he is, the more binding is his obligation to serve the interests of his institution loyally. Doubtless it is true enough that the journalist who serves society best serves his paper best in the long run; but it is not necessarily true in the short run, for it is possible to bankrupt a newspaper in a very short time. A bankrupt newspaper, like a dead liberal, is of no further use to anybody. Therefore, its first duty is to stay alive. The obvious means to that end is to fight for survival of the group to which it belongs.

Hence, when newspapers strive to protect the interests of industrial corporations, the fact is no proof that they are either dishonest or disloyal. It does, however, reduce their effectiveness as promoters of national unity.

However, a means remains open to them whereby they may reasonably expect to become powerful agents—possibly the most powerful—in bringing order out of chaos. That means is simply to realize clearly and exercise fully the duty of freedom of the press. Please note the choice of words. I said the "duty," not the "right" of freedom of the press. Newspapers possess no right in freedom of the press. It is the readers who possess the right. The newspapers have only the duty of making that right effective.

Why does the Constitution forbid any abridgment, even by Congress, of freedom of the press? Was it based on the Constitution makers' high regard for the character of printers? "The printers can never leave us in a state of perfect rest and union of opinion," said Thomas Jefferson. "They would be no longer useful and would have to go to the plow."

That was a mild opinion by comparison with what other Founding Fathers said and what Jefferson said at other times. But it disposes of the idea that the press was expected to produce national unity. Nevertheless, the clause stands in the organic law, and it was defended even by Hamilton. True, he saw no need for explicit statement, but that was because he considered freedom of the press inherent in the American system itself.

No rational man contends that the system was established for the benefit of printers. It is the people's government and it was devised not to protect, but to demolish all rights but the people's rights. Freedom of the press is the people's right. Under it, newspapers enjoy immunity from censorship only because that immunity was considered essential to the people's welfare. The First Amendment, therefore, simply delegates to the press the duty of insuring the people the enjoyment of one of their rights. Only as long as it discharges this duty is it entitled to any special position in law or morals.

The conditions under which that duty may be discharged have altered radically since 1787. In those days the policy of *laissez faire* was much more practical than it is today. When all the equipment necessary to start a newspaper was, in the parlance of the craft, a Washington handpress and a shirttail full of type, competition was a fairly reliable guarantee against the imposition of any informal, private censorship. Hence, if a formal, public censorship were forever prohibited, none could exist.

That safeguard no longer is effective. Today the investment required to establish a newspaper in a large city runs into prodigious sums, and the expense of maintaining one is staggering. That expense is a charge on the business activity of the city. In recent years it has grown so large that very few American cities are able to support more than one newspaper. The business tends more and more to become a natural monopoly, for the same reason that telephone and streetcar services are natural monopolies. The communities simply cannot afford competitive services.

The law recognized long ago that when any business becomes a natural monopoly, it changes its character. It is no longer exclusively a private enterprise, but becomes affected with a public interest and, therefore, subject to public regulation.

How are you going to subject newspapers to regulation without setting up a formal, public censorship—the very thing that the Constitution specifically forbids? That is the question that neither press nor government has as yet been able to answer explicitly.

At the same time, an implicit answer is already being given by certain shrewd and farsighted publishers. It is a somewhat vague and uncertain answer, therefore not pleasing to logicians and precisionists. It is simply an effort to forestall any strong demand for regulation by actually maintaining the freedom of the reader by discharging fully the duty of the freedom of the press.

The newspaper purveys information and opinion. That is to say, it reports what men are doing and what they are thinking. As regards information, the newspapers have achieved the effect of competition paradoxically by accommodation. That is to say, the great news services supply news to papers of all parties and all sections. It is, therefore, impossible to slant the news in any specific direction without offending some of the customers. So the news is not consciously and deliberately colored. Colored it is without doubt, sometimes, but only because it is handled by fallible human beings. Fallibility of mortal man is not to be corrected by regulation or legislation.

As regards opinion, in a great many one-newspaper towns, the publisher is making an honest effort to discharge his duty as a proprietor of a monopoly by the institution of the columnist. It is not a perfect expedient. The majestic wrath of the White House directed repeatedly at columnists is well understood, if not altogether appreciated by publishers.

Has anyone as yet devised a better means of acquainting the readers of one newspaper with many, not to say all shades of opinion? Observers, especially Europeans, are frequently amazed and sometimes amused by the blatant inconsistency of an American newspaper that presents on its editorial page a column or two taking a very definite attitude, and then publishing, perhaps on the same page, two or three signed columns flatly denying everything the newspaper has said. But this inconsistency of statement is a small price to pay for the vast and more important consistent support of the freedom of the reader to learn what opinions are abroad in the land. The fact that to the publishers some of them are silly opinions is irrelevant. As long as they are neither libelous nor obscene, it is not merely his right, it is his duty to permit his readers to know of their existence.

For emphasis, let me repeat that I do not maintain that this is the most satisfactory solution of the problem. It is a solution of sorts. Its more spectacularly unsatisfactory phases are due rather to the quality of the columnists rather than to the defects of the system. Nor is the real objection to the columnists so much the fact that some of them propagate wrong opinions, as the fact that some of them propagate no opinions at all, but devote their space to triviality and vulgarity.

This situation is open to correction by the publisher. A man of good sense and good taste can find today a commentator of almost any shade of political opinion, who is neither vulgar nor trivial. Hence, it may be assumed that a man who publishes worthless columns is simply a bad editor.

It is true that the obligation to publish a diversity of opinion is not universally recognized by the press. As recently as 1925, the *Wall Street Journal* said editorially, "A newspaper is a private enterprise owing nothing to the public which grants it no franchise. It is, therefore, affected with no public interest. It is emphatically the property of its owner who is selling a manufactured product at his own risk." That attitude still has its adherents. Some of them are very successful and very powerful.

It cannot be said, therefore, that the American daily-newspaper press is as yet an agency of national unity. On the contrary, important sections of it are strong influences toward disunity. But is there a single institution in the land of which as much cannot be said? In business and in politics there are certainly recalcitrant elements. We have fanatical religious sects whose chief aspiration and highest happiness seem to be sowing discord. The trend of the group is the important thing.

Certainly the trend of those American newspapers that are moving at all is in the direction of recognition of their obligation to furnish their readers with a true report of opinion as well as a true report of events.

How can this serve national unity? At first glance it would seem not to serve it at all. On the contrary, by advertising it emphasizes all our differences. As a matter of fact, its success depends entirely upon the soundness of American political philosophy.

"The way to prevent such a thing as Shay's rebellion," said Jefferson, "is to give them—the people—full information of their affairs through the channel of the public papers, and to contrive that those papers shall penetrate the whole mass of the people."

If he was wrong, then our whole system is wrong from the beginning and nothing can be expected of it. But if he was right, then full information conveyed to all the people will produce a judgment sound enough to be tolerable to a majority. As it is their own judgment, not manufactured for them by some superior authority, they will support it heartily enough to keep the rebellious in order. This is about as complete a national unity as we can expect to achieve— perhaps as complete as we ought to seek to achieve. A dead-level uniformity of opinion in the United States would be a calamity of the first order. A unanimity general enough to make violent revolt against it hopeless, will achieve the maintenance of public order. Within the limits of public order, the more discussion and debate we have, the better are our chances of hitting upon improvements in the life of the nation that will enrich and enlarge the existence of every man.

The press, therefore, should make no effort to achieve national unity by exhortation and admonition. It is in no position to exhort or admonish, since it is a special economic, social, and political interest, one of the battlers among many battlers for survival. Its duty is to inform, not partially or one-sidedly, but to the fullest extent that its physical resources and energies admit.

It has a right to the expression of its own opinion, but no right to impose an effective censorship on the expression of contrary opinions by employing its monopolistic position to that end. Indeed, the proposition is more than a negative one. The press has no right to impose a censorship, and it has, on the other hand, a duty to try to acquaint its readers with all shades of opinion.

To discharge this duty, the duty of the freedom of the press rightly understood as the freedom of the reader, is the best contribution it can make to the success of the democratic theory and the unity of the nation.

DISCUSSION

QUESTION: The lowest criminal in America gets his day in court; he is arraigned and he may have the most skillful lawyer he can get to put up his defense. Why is it inconsistent for one page of a newspaper to be an arena where that can be done, rather than one newspaper being the plaintiff and the other the defense?

Is it inconsistent for one page of a newspaper to be an arena where both sides are heard? Before we went to war with Germany and Japan should the views of the most powerful exponent of their attitude have been distributed throughout America?

MR. JOHNSON: You mean editorial expression?

QUESTION: I don't care how it is expressed—just so you get a chance to know what their point is.

MR. JOHNSON: I spoke of the direct and conscious molder of public opinion. I was speaking especially of editorial expression which has the authority of the paper behind it.

It was measured a while back by the Gallup people. Mr. Aldgate, the fellow who thinks up the questions for the Gallup Poll, wrote a book in which he explained how they became interested in that. They tried to pick out a field in which it could be measured. They picked on the territory around Chicago. They did not take Chicago itself because there are competitive newspapers there.

In downstate Illinois and over in Iowa, and in various places, *The Chicago Tribune* is unquestionably the dominant newspaper. *The Chicago Tribune* developed its powerful isolationist attitude after the outbreak of the war in Europe—that is to say, after 1939. As it happened, the Gallup Poll had made three surveys throughout that territory touching on the international situation. Therefore, before Pearl Harbor, but after the war had begun, they figured that there was a good place to measure the effect of public opinion. There was a newspaper that has taken a particularly strong attitude on a subject which we have measured before. Now we will go back and measure it again and see what the change is.

So they made three careful surveys. They came out almost identical. The best change they could figure was one-and-one-half per cent. Well, now, they admit that the factor of error in a Gallup Poll runs to three per cent. Therefore, what they found was no perceptible change whatever. That was a dominant newspaper in its own region, on a subject in which everybody had an interest. It had no effect.

QUESTION: When *The New York Times* came out announcing it was in favor of the election of Mr. Roosevelt, was it the editor himself who was responsible for that opinion or was he expressing the opinion of, shall we call it, the corporation?

MR. JOHNSON: In a modern newspaper the editor does not express his own opinion, and usually he does not express that of any other one man on a matter of real importance. If a question is one of the highest importance there is always a consultation among editorial writers. If it is a matter of great importance such as which political party to support, the publisher is certainly called in, the news executives; everybody of any considerable importance in the organization participates in a final decision.

There may be some exceptions. I do not know if Mr. Marshall Field writes exactly what he thinks in the Chicago *Sun*. Generally speaking, on a large newspaper the general opinion is the resultant of half a dozen opinions thrashed out in a conference. It does not make any difference who happens to write the result. That is just a matter of style. But the opinion therein is the opinion of that group.

Incidentally, there is something about that that is weak. I do not know why, but the average reader is much more impressed if he attaches a personality to an expression. He picks up a column and reads it, and it happens to be by Walter Lippmann. "Well, all right, I'll see what he says." On the next page, this is *The New York Herald Tribune*. Well, who is *The New York Herald Tribune?* The fellow never saw it. It is a group. It is a somewhat amorphous outfit. But this man Lippmann, he knows. He may not agree with him at all. Nevertheless, the fellow is interesting; he will see what Lippmann has to say about this. Even if he is busy, he will see what Lippmann has to say, and perhaps may not see what the *Herald Tribune* has to say at all.

There is something in the human mind, in the average reader's mind that responds to a personality. It does not respond to the most logically, carefully, brilliantly reasoned argument that just stands out as an argument and not the expression of any one man.

Back in the old days, in the times of personal journalism, people used to read everything in *The New York Sun* as the expression of Charles A. Dana, or in the *Tribune* as Horace Greeley in person. Four times out of five it was not either Dana or Greeley. Some fellow in the office wrote the editorial. Nevertheless, those men stood out, and the reader attached that personality to them. They were tremendously powerful.

Newspapermen say personal journalism has gone out. That is the great myth of the profession, that personal journalism has disappeared. What they mean is that journalism has disappeared in the sense of being a molder of public opinion. When the personality went, so did the power. The newspaper now molds public opinion only by reporting the event. If a newspaper's reports are accurate, everybody knows they are accurate, and of course it has a powerful effect. But the effect is that of truth itself, not the effect of the argument. The people who mold public opinion are the men who are known to the public. They are strong. I think a good many of these commentators can swing many thousands of votes at any time. The only measurement that ever was made was that by the Gallup Poll, and it did not reveal any editorial influence whatever.

QUESTION: I wonder what the possible future is of endowed newspapers —if that is a good term for it—I mean the kind of newspaper we have in *PM,* which does not have to show a business profit. It is not a prejudiced newspaper, but a liberal newspaper. Is there any future for additional newspapers of that kind?

Mr. Johnson: Of course there is a future for it as long as the endowment holds out. I do not think the endowed newspaper is a necessity. If the commercial newspaper will recognize its duty to present all sides—not its right, but its duty—whether it is done by employed columnists or whether it is done by careful reporting—if you can pick up your morning newspaper and be perfectly certain that, by the time you have read it through, you have a pretty good idea of what all sides are thinking, maybe you do not have to have an endowed newspaper. You can be perfectly satisfied. On its editorial page the newspaper may never say a word you agree with. If in its other columns it gives you an accurate summary not only of the events but also of the thought of the country and the neighborhood, you can very well let it express its opinion even if you do not agree with it. I think that is what most people are doing.

You realize that New York is in a very special position. New York is so large it is able to maintain a competitive press, but it is almost the only city in the country that still does so. Until the establishment of *The Sun,* Chicago was a one-morning-newspaper town; Baltimore has one morning newspaper. It has come to the place now where a two-morning-newspaper city is the exception. I can remember within my own lifetime when any city that had as many as 30,000 people had at least two newspapers. When I was a boy, Raleigh, N.C., maintained two and sometimes three. The population of the city was less than 25,000.

Today it cannot be done. It is an enormous expense to gather the news. So much more news is presented than ever was before. Gathering it is expensive. Printing it is expensive. Distributing it is expensive. All that money has to come out of the town one way or another, either through subscriptions or advertising. The towns just can't put it up.

Question: Mr. Johnson, do you think that the Gallup Poll can still be taken seriously after Mr. Gallup's own admission that he corrected the figures that were demonstrated by his poll?

Mr. Johnson: To base any sort of judgment on one sample is extremely unscientific. But if only one sample exists in all the world, you have to take it into consideration. This is the only measurement of its kind, so far as I know, that has ever been made with anything like care. It made a great impression because it tended to corroborate political events. There is no doubt that the bulk of the newspapers for twelve mortal years have been fighting the Administration, and they have not got anywhere.

Obviously, that particular kind of editorial opinion was having very little effect. This thing refers not to party politics but to the international situation, and it shows no more effect. They thought, too, that this was a good thing to try the sample on, because party passions were not particularly involved, and they thought they would get a better measurement.

Still, I have to admit it is only one sample and it is completely inconclusive, because the results were all within the factor of error. Therefore, they cannot make any statement.

QUESTION: If the trend in American cities of large proportions is toward one newspaper, what guarantee is there that the newspaper will perform the duty which you think they should perform? What will hold them to the performance of that duty?

MR. JOHNSON: Well, there is no guarantee. I think the answer to the question is simply this: If the trend toward monopoly continues and if there is no effort to present a diversity of opinion, then public regulation is as certain as sunrise; it just has to come.

QUESTION: Mr. Johnson, if the increased use of radio and possibly television will make the news value greater than on the printed page, will the function of the newspaper change from news gathering to perhaps reflected opinion?

MR. JOHNSON: The principal effect of the radio on the newspaper has been a very salutary one. It has saved them a lot of money. A terrible expense in producing a newspaper is in speed. That is to say, the expense increases in geometrical progression with speed. When the newspapers had to get on the streets instantly with any important piece of news, they wasted money by shovelfuls. Today they cannot get on the street; radio is there first—no possibility of beating them. Therefore, they can move more slowly. It has saved them a lot of money—a great deal of money. It has not hurt the circulation at all.

X

WHAT BUSINESS CAN DO

EDWARD L. BERNAYS

Public opinion is characterized by low or high visibility. In that respect, public opinion may be compared to an iceberg. Like an iceberg, it may be submerged, invisible, and potentially dangerous, or it may be highly visible.

Vital and important situations do not always have high visibility with the public. Racial and religious tensions, for example, have low visibility for a number of reasons. In the first place, they are screened by social taboos which people wish to avoid. The average citizen is far more interested in, and feels more at ease with pleasant matters, whether they are gardening or sports. Moreover, racial and religious tensions call for thought-provoking treatment in print. A glance at the typical newspaper reveals that the preponderance of news and editorial space is not given over to "think pieces."

Obviously, low visibility of any issue has its effects on public opinion. It makes it difficult to articulate or crystallize public opinion into constructive social and legal action on that issue. Democratic leaders have an obligation to increase the visibility on the race issue. When that is done, we can trust democracy to deal with the problem.

By the very nature of a democracy, its leaders are constantly changing. They can be rejected at the will of the public. They can move only as fast as their followers will keep pace with them. This is a complicating element in dealing with race-relations problems.

This was brought home to me very forcibly only a few weeks ago when public-relations steps that we advised helped stop a race riot in a certain border-state city. Leaders must work through existing channels of communication which, in turn, depend upon mass support. Experiences in the border-state city referred to show what reaction papers and other organs of expression have to these problems. One newspaper executive, when asked to run stories that might stop the crisis from developing, said to me: "I can promise you, Mr. Bernays, that we will cover the riots if there are enough deaths. But, it isn't a story, you know, if only a couple of fellows get knocked around. And it isn't a story before sufficient deaths make it newsworthy!"

"What about dealing with the conflict in terms of an issue?" I asked him.

"That is a hot potato and we'd rather not handle it," was his reply.

"Why?"

"Don't forget our public," he said.

Many obstacles stand in the way of solving race problems through our existing media of communication. If you go to the broadcasting systems, you find, with few exceptions, an unwritten code in deference not to the majority of the population, but to Southerners. Thus, radio networks preserve the stereotypes and the clichés about the Negro, and other racial groups for that matter.

It is a very encouraging sign that some of the ablest writers associated with the Writers' War Board recently organized to study these stereotypes on the radio and in other media. Recognizing the role of the writer in molding public opinion, this group hopes to create more representative and honest characterizations.

Nonetheless, in local areas, editorial treatment of possible sore spots in race relations follows too often a definite pattern. This was expressed to me in the statement, "This is a hot potato. It isn't handled until it is so hot that it explodes. When the explosion comes, that makes news." Of course, by that time, the damage has been done.

Leaders must work with and through the existing social forces that affect these channels of communication which, in turn, affect public opinion. Improvements in race relations will depend on the role these forces play in using social pressure for constructive ends— for the prevention of such explosions as riots and demonstrations.

Race tension, particularly between Negroes and whites, has been accentuated by the war. On a recent trip, I talked to a man from Dallas, Texas, who was sitting next to me on the train. I asked him how long he had lived in Dallas. "I have been there about ten years," he said. "I married a Dallas girl and I am in her father's business."

"Where did you go to school?"

"In a college in New York."

Then his wife chimed in: "You know, we had the oddest adventure in New York. One day we went out to Westchester on the railroad. We were sitting near the front of the car and suddenly noticed that a 'nigger' was sitting right behind us! Hubby was just going to hit him over the head—"

"Why?" I asked the man.

"Well, you know, in Texas we don't have those fellows up so near the front," he answered. "We have them in the back of the car."

I said, "Well, you learned to be a Southerner pretty soon, didn't you?"

He said, "I certainly did!"

"What do you think about Dallas?" I asked.

"It will be a fine place when we kill a thousand 'niggers,'" he answered.

I said, "That seems pretty unsound when we are fighting this war for democracy."

His answer was: "They have to keep their place."

I was in Detroit before the great riot occurred there and the air was filled with the same tension. I remarked to a taxi driver, "This is a nice town you're in."

"It's nice," he said, "but it will be a lot nicer when we kill the 'nigger' GIs that are coming back."

I watched him carefully during our conversation. Here was a man ordinarily mild and nonaggressive. However, any key word or idea on Negro-white relations started high tension within him. So violent was the tension that he could easily have become a member of a lynching mob.

I want to give you a picture of these tensions, because I am going to try to outline an objective toward which to move in helping to lessen them.

I have here a monthly summary of events and trends in race relations, an index that is published by the Julius Rosenwald Fund. This is for August, 1943, through July, 1944. Observe the sources of tension in the situations which it lists:

Armed Forces' soldier violence—Birmingham, Alabama; Camp Philips, Kansas; Georgia; Camp Tyson, Tennessee; South Carolina; Fayetteville, North Carolina; and so on.

Demonstrations, discriminations: Atlantic City, Brooklyn, New York, Louisiana, Baltimore, Norfolk, St. Louis, Seafarer's Union, Philadelphia; Detroit, Cincinnati, Chicago.

Education: Teachers' salaries, Fair Employment Practice Committee, Boiler Makers' Union, Capital Transit Company; Chicago, Northwestern University.

Public health and housing: a long list of discriminations.

Industry and labor: a whole page of them.

Hate strikes: Akron, Baltimore, Detroit, Brooklyn, New York, and so on.

These widespread tensions permeate educational work, labor, transportation, and every other field of activity.

I found in talking to both Negroes and whites of all social stratifications, in the border-state city I referred to before, that these tensions were highly accentuated by conditions resulting from the war. Economic insecurity loomed large in importance. The whites of the lower income groups had economic insecurity—they feared that the Negroes might get their jobs. In turn, the Negroes were afraid that they might be displaced by white workers.

I was greatly impressed with the Negro leaders. They were highly objective and recognized that that was the time to consolidate gains in improving their status. They felt that, if they did not, it would be difficult to do it when the GI's returned.

Race tension in this area was accentuated by the impact of war, and by the goals emphasized to the people for the war. Freedom, equality, and justice were emphasized by the Atlantic Charter. These ideals were belied by situations existing in the city. This was evident in many phases of daily life from a bus company refusing employment to Negroes, to Jim Crowism in the schools.

All the necessary components of an explosion are here.

My introduction to the race problem occurred many years ago, in 1921. I was asked to go to Atlanta by Oswald Garrison Villard, James Weldon Johnson, and Mary White Ovington. The National Association for the Advancement of Colored People was holding its first conference in the South, and I was asked to handle the publicity. I remember this scene vividly. A Julius Rosenwald Y.M.C.A. telephone operator would not give a Negro woman from Iowa her home telephone number. She was not . . . "going to give any 'nigger' a long distance telephone connection."

Who is going to bear the burden of leadership in dealing with these problems?

Who is going to accept the burden of speeding up social change?

How is that leadership going to prevent aggression and bloodshed on both sides? How will it bring about that unity so important in maintaining and strengthening our democracy?

Professor MacIver, in his books, has listed these forces. Let us analyze them.

First, there are the social workers. They have borne the burden to a great extent thus far. The social worker represents an important and valuable social force. Of necessity, however, very few social workers have the necessary leverages, or the skills, or experience in influencing the public to a new course of action.

Social workers have not the effective machinery to create high visibility for an issue and swing the public with them. When dealing with individuals on a personal basis, they can appeal to kindness, humanity, and intelligence in counteracting existing conditions. There it ends. Reviewing what has been accomplished through social work, it is clear that there is not enough power here greatly to affect the race problem. And then, too, social workers reflect the point of view of the economic interests on which they are dependent.

Review of religion as a social force will reveal that important contributions have been made to the furthering of better race relations. These contributions have resulted from the efforts of a few, rather than from the great breadth and length of the church body in the

United States. In small communities, particularly, religious leaders obviously can represent only the patterns, the folkways, or the culture of their communities.

I went to see a distinguished bishop in a border city and was received graciously. I said to him, "Your part in aligning your communicants with this issue and tackling this crisis situation would add great strength to our cause." This was a matter of ending certain discriminations against Negroes in a minor field—Jim Crowism in restaurants.

"Mr. Bernays, why pick issues like that?" he replied. "Why not a broad issue like housing?"

"Bishop, I didn't pick the issue," I said, "but I know from their standpoint that it is a vital issue, because it represents a principle. Now, what does it mean from your standpoint?"

He said: "These things are always so complicated. It is so difficult to make a decision. You know what these people in our town think about the subject, how touchy they are, and what the history of this community is."

He said he would think it over. I believe he is still thinking it over.

I asked an important preacher in the same border city what his organization was doing about race tensions in his community.

"We have made great progress," he said. "We exchange pulpits once a year with Negro and white ministers. But I'll tell you of a clever trick I use in making the exchange."

"What is it?" I asked.

He said, "When we put a Negro preacher in the white pulpit we don't tell the congregation in advance."

I am aware of the good work accomplished by the Federal Council of Churches of Christ in America and other religious institutions today. However, they do not have the power to alter a current that is running strongly at this time.

What about education as a social force in racial situations? One Catholic university in a border city had never admitted Negroes. The second-in-command of that university wrote to a number of enlightened members of the community on this question. The response was immediate and vigorous in favor of admitting them. The university today enrolls Negro students.

The technique used by that university executive was a sound and decisive one for social purposes. Let me emphasize, though, that it is not used often. It is easier to drift with the tide.

Here in New York City, Negro children are not segregated by law. But the schools in Harlem are definitely for Negro children and the facilities are none too good.

In education, as in religion, there is the same lack of leverage in effectiveness of bringing about change. The educational authorities more often reflect public opinion than lead it.

On another one of my trips to the same city, I engaged a taxi driver in conversation. Taxi drivers are pretty good indices of public opinion. I remarked, "It seems to me that this is a great town for children to grow up in."

"Right now it is," he said, "because we have Jim Crow in the public schools."

"That's strange," I said. "I just read that a nearby Catholic university is definitely admitting Negro students."

"Listen, Mister," he glared, "I'll take my daughter out of the public school, and put her in a parochial school if any changes are made in this town. Parochial schools don't admit them."

The professions make up an important social force. We find liberals in this group naturally. Liberals' thoughts and ideals do not always translate themselves into social action. Liberals often are reserved and not too practical. They often rely on lawmaking for social change. They forget that laws can be nullified by public opinion. Civil-rights laws help, but public opinion must back them for proper enforcement. The other day, for example, a leading New York hotel was asked to rent a hall for a meeting of Negroes and whites. The banquet manager said, "How many Negroes?"

"I think about sixty per cent Negroes."

"That's bad," he said.

In other words, it was too much. "Too much" had a moral value in terms of bad—*bad* for business, despite the Civil-Rights law in New York State.

Though women's organizations are always anxious to do their part, they, too, are seriously handicapped. Generally, they are on the right side of the fence but they propagandize mainly to people who believe as they do, instead of getting out and talking to those who do not.

They should of course carry their message as the gospel is carried— to the unbelievers. They should talk to everybody—from the merchants' association to unions—anyone who discriminates against the Negro.

Government, especially the Federal branch, acts as if it were walking a tightrope on this problem. There are, of course, courageous leaders in executive positions—Henry A. Wallace, who is very much concerned with these problems. Harold Ickes is courageous. There are men like John Collier, long in the office of Indian Affairs, and Abe Fortas, Undersecretary of the Interior, and others who are tremendously interested.

When the Federal Government is asked to take action in a local crisis, what is the Government's answer apt to be?

They say, "Have you forgotten about States Rights in this country? You wouldn't want Washington to interfere in a local situation. Of course, if there is a riot and many people are killed, we will send in the troops. You can rest assured that everything then will be all right."

Government on local levels is likely to be no better than the ambitions of the local top man. In New York, there is a Mayor's Committee on Unity. A representative of this committee came to my office. "What have you done?" I asked him.

"Oh, not much," he said. "The committee isn't interested in anything but research. As an example of our findings, we found that the worst cuts of meat are sold in Harlem. In addition, they are more expensive than good cuts."

"That is a good news story," I said. "Are you going to use it?"

"I don't know," he answered. "The committee may not want to use it."

I said, "Are you going to do anything about that?"

"Well, I'd like to," was his response.

"Why not get the committee to do something?" I asked.

"One man on the committee resigned because the other members were going to come out against the Ives-Quinn Anti-Discrimination Bill," he said.

"That looks like a poor committee," I told him. "Why not resign, yourself, and get some publicity?"

"That's a good idea," was his reply. "I'll think about that."

It is evident from a review of what local governments do that we cannot expect much from most city governments.

What does this analysis lead up to? All the social forces that we have listed are handicapped in meeting the racial problems brought about by the psychological and economic insecurities that will presumably come with war's end. Large numbers of veterans, including almost a million Negro servicemen, will have to be re-absorbed into civilian life. The process, inevitably marked by frustration, aggression, and distress, will make for even greater tension between Negro and white.

What approach can we make toward meeting this problem? What group can we look to for leadership? The burden of leadership must be, I believe, assumed by business. There is no other social force that has sufficient strength to change the shape of the existing social pattern. Other social forces are held back by prejudice, by fear, by those who control them.

What branch of business can we look to for help? Certainly not small business. Small business is worried about itself. In its attitude toward the Negro, it is caught between the cross fire of the prejudiced and those who are not. So it plays safe—on a *laissez-faire* basis.

What about big business? The development of our entire business structure depends on peace—social and industrial peace. This calls for sound consumer and employee relations, and with the community as a whole.

It is up to the American business leader in his own enlightened self-interest to assume responsibility in this situation. From the standpoint of all American business, the Detroit riots were a black eye to the great American industries located there. The public rightly felt that business should have assumed leadership in preventing such occurrences.

Business has highly effective tools for mass persuasion. There are many evidences in this room, of the persuasive ability of business. What you wear is testimony to the power of business to form your habits. Business is the greatest and most skillful user of mass-persuasion tools. Over $2,386,000,000 a year is spent in advertising alone.

The answer of how to deal with the problem is so logical and simple that it is surprising it has not been done before. It is to enlist the active interest of the most powerful business forces—

(1) The investment bankers. Ten or twenty leading investment bankers can bring enormous influence to bear on American big business.

(2) The heads of the large corporations who employ thousands of workers.

Investment bankers must realize that, in order to protect their stake in business, they must insure the peaceful running of business, and peaceful conduct of the consumer community. There can be no peace while nine men out of ten may be aligned against the tenth— the Negro—with a growing resentment on the part of that tenth of the population. A community that is torn by riots and racial struggle is a bad business risk. Once the banker understands this elementary fact, he will decide that it is up to him to do something to remove the cause of frictions destructive to good will, to revenue, to growth. He will study methods of constructive treatment for group tensions, and he will find a stimulating mass of research and practice to guide him.

He will call into conference the industrial leaders in the areas of trouble and explain the inescapable financial and industrial logic of the situation. Together, finance and industry will assume the leadership that is rightfully theirs, and will utilize the best means of integrating the Negro into our economic life, giving him the freedom and right to work that are essential to a smooth-running business machine and to our Democracy—both.

To sum up briefly, there are great leverages in:

(a) Economic pressures

(b) The force and power of millions of workers

(c) The influence of large corporations on the small businessman by establishing precedents of behavior.

These leverages are related directly to the profit motive. If the members of any group interested in improving the situation will recognize the strength of these leverages, and work with this group, the results should be effective. The force and power of this group can play a vital role both by itself and as a catalyst for other groups of good will in helping solve what Myrdal so rightly called "The American Dilemma."

DISCUSSION

MEMBER: Certainly no one would take issue with Mr. Bernays, that it would be a good thing for business to take a hand in this matter. His optimism and utter confidence, however, in business being able to handle it and having such tremendous power, might be open to question on the basis of a number of experiences. One that I can think of is the attitude that business took in several recent elections in the past eight years. It appeared that big business that dominated radio and newspapers had one point of view and did whatever it could to persuade the American public to adopt that point of view. However, as results showed, a great part of the American public refused to be influenced by these efforts.

Pursuing another direction, I ask, Mr. Bernays, whether we can blithely dismiss the influence of organized religion, such as the Federal Council and other groups, and of organized labor? Labor, through PAC, played an important role in the recent election. Can we dismiss the power of the church and the unions in affecting public opinions?

MR. BERNAYS: I do not—and did not dismiss the influence of the church. I tried to bring out that the church was hampered by the communities in which it works. The influence of the Federal Council of Churches cannot be underestimated, but it does not appear to be powerful enough to solve the problems we are faced with today.

Obviously, the efforts of labor are very important. The CIO, particularly through the efforts of Philip Murray, has done much to effect change. On the other hand, it may interest you to know that in some communities, there have been breaks in labor's ranks from the mandates of the national unions. For example, there are instances where union workers repudiated their leadership on the matter of integrating the Negro into the shops. Had there been, in these communities, employer support of union officials, the results might have been different. This support can come only when there is awakened interest on the part of businessmen who recognize the importance of the problem, and who will study and act on it as the American Management Association has done.

MEMBER: We all here are deeply indebted, or should be, to Mr. Bernays for having brought into high visibility a fact that is not well known, not as well known as it should be in this country: Had he been analyzing the destinies of France, it would not have been necessary to emphasize high visibility of the controlling factor. Specifically, I am referring to the 200 families that dominated the country. In keen semantic dissection and analyses of forces within the United States, Mr. Bernays has brought out very clearly that which we are reluctant to admit, that a small group of investment bankers and industrial organizations are in control of the country's affairs—

MR. BERNAYS: In part.

MEMBER: Major part. Certainly, when it comes to changing the mores, they affect many things. My personal experience in appealing to these individuals might be illustrated by one, perhaps, not particularly apt experience: Some years ago, I discussed this problem with the president of a large utility organization employing 35,000 people. In answer to my question, he said: "Why, we don't discriminate." He rang for George and George came in. He said to his colored man, "George, how long have you been with me?"

George replied, "Ever since you were secretary to Theodore Roosevelt."

He said, "Of course we don't discriminate here. Here is a very clear illustration of the fact that we do not exclude Negroes from our service."

MR. BERNAYS: I have emphasized in my talk the need of objectives, themes, strategy, planning, organization, and tactics in dealing with the public. There is one other element. Timing becomes highly important. The campaign we are discussing now might not have been very effective years ago. Today, we are faced with different circumstances. The social consciousness of business and other leaders has been highly developed by events that have taken place. It seems to me time will bring further social consciousness of business and make the campaign increasingly effective.

XI

WHAT THE COURTS CAN DO

CIVIL RIGHTS IN VERBAL JEOPARDY

BY

WALTON HALE HAMILTON

It is hardly seemly that a right of man should depend upon the turn of a legal phrase. But a right is what a court declares it to be; and so long as rights are grand abstractions, unless the courts put their sanctions behind them, they cannot escape the hazards which inhere in the ways of the law. For, although the law, like the rights it protects, may be from heaven, it is administered upon earth, and in its judgments cannot rise above human wisdom. And judges are themselves lawyers, quite prone to be taken captive by the practice of their craft and not immune to being taken in by vested interests in their own cleverly contrived arguments. A single story, so well documented that a layman may spell it out for himself, reveals the perils of the mind amid which our cherished and not so ancient liberties are set. The drama has a central theme—the right of the Texas Negro to vote in the Democratic primary. There are four great acts; the scene throughout is the Supreme Court of the United States.

On a certain Monday in March, 1928, the Supreme Court, according to its custom, was handing down decisions from its high bench in the Capitol. When his turn came, Mr. Justice Holmes casually remarked, "I am authorized to deliver the judgment of the court in the case of *Nixon* v. *Herndon*." [1] It was a notorious cause, and the audience which packed the old courtroom was immediately at attention. For the legislature of Texas had by statute decreed that

[1] 273 U.S. 536.

143

no Negro should vote in the Democratic primary; and a certain Dr. Nixon, of El Paso, resolved to subject the act to the ordeal at law. So he appeared at the polling place, pleaded Texas and United States citizenship, demanded a ballot, was courteously refused, pleaded a denial of civil rights, and brought suit for damages against the election commissioners. The local court stood by the state legislature; and Nixon took an appeal to—in words once employed by Charles Evans Hughes—"the court of last resort and ultimate error."

The very fact that Holmes was speaking for the court was a giveaway before he read a word from the document before him. But if the result was not in doubt, even those skilled in judicial prophecy could not have foretold the line of argument by which he was to reach his conclusion. For the case had been argued as if it concerned the Fifteenth Amendment, Nixon's attorney insisting that no state could deny a person suffrage because of "race, color, or previous condition of servitude," and the champion of the legislature arguing that a primary was a party—and therefore a private—affair quite beyond the reach of the amendment. Justice was doubtless with Nixon, but the legal going was a little rough; for a little while before the Court had excused a candidate for the United States Senate, who had been a more generous spender than the corrupt practices act allowed, on the ground that the party primary was "antecedent to" but "no part of" the election.[2] But Holmes, by a bold move, waved the precedent away. He waved aside the Fifteenth Amendment and invoked the Fourteenth which was quite free from embarrassing interpretations. That act accomplished—he was far too canny to advertise what he had done—the rest was easy. For he was then free, in the very best dialectical manner, to insist that the right to vote in the Democratic primary was a part of a man's liberty which a state was forbidden by the Constitution to abridge or deny. For a unanimous court he found it hard "to imagine a more direct infringement of the Fourteenth Amendment" whose very purpose was to secure "the equal protection of the laws." In a word, it was "too clear for

[2] *Newberry* v. *U.S.*, 256 U.S. 232. The vote had been five to four; a change of one vote and *Nixon* v. *Herndon* would have been disposed of by referral to the Fifteenth Amendment.

extended argument that color" could not be made "the basis for classification." The court rose gloriously to the occasion; but whether its writ would run in Texas was in the mind of Holmes an open question. For, when he had laid the opinion down, he remarked with an ironical chuckle, "I know our good friends the Negroes of Texas will rejoice to know that they now possess at the primary all the rights which heretofore they have exercised at the general election."

The off-the-record remark was prophecy as well as political summary. The legislature of Texas resolved to have its own way—and yet to respect the judgment of the Court. It accepted the Supreme Court's appeal of its own statute, and in its stead solemnly entrusted to the executive committee of the political party the task of determining the proper qualifications of voters in its primary. The executive committee, then, exercising its own independent judgment, ruled that Negroes were ineligible to participate in the political process by which the Democratic slate was selected. Once more Dr. Nixon took his civic rights to the poll; once more they were politely waived and found wanting; once more he essayed his law and brought suit against the election officials. Again the local court stood by the "white primary"; and again the cause was taken to the Supreme Court.

When in due course Mr. Justice Cardozo announced, "I am authorized to deliver the judgment of this Court in the case of *Nixon* v. *Condon*," [3] it was evident that all was well along the Potomac even if not along the Rio Grande. It was, however, a harder task which Holmes's successor faced; and the victory, though glorious, was left insecure. For a time argument marched nicely; and it reached its result before its vitality was spent. The power exercised by the executive committee, reasoned Cardozo, was not "inherent" in the party but had been "conferred by statute." Hence the executive committee had acted, not on its own behalf or in behalf of the Democracy of Texas, but as an agent to which the legislature of Texas had delegated its power. Hence its act, which was clearly an abridgment of civil liberty, was the act of the state and as such forbidden by the Constitution. The Herndon case was controlling; for "an identity of

[3] 286 U.S. 73.

result" had been achieved "by a diversity of method." But the argument floundered before it was finished; for Cardozo admitted that, had the power to exclude been "inherent" rather than statutory, had the decision to exclude been that of the party *convention* and not of its executive committee, the court would have been hard put to it to outlaw the denial of the liberty as the act of the state. The "ifs" are, of course, no part of the Court's decision but they are rather pointed hints to the state of Texas as to how a forbidden objective may be lawfully attained.[4]

So broad a hint was not to be overlooked by such men of the world as made up the Texas legislature. They lost no time in erasing from the statute books all that could be construed as instructions to a delegate. Then the party on its own, by act of its state convention, decreed that henceforth no Negro was to participate in the Democratic primary. By this time Dr. Nixon seems to have been worn out in an attempt lawfully to make good his liberty, for the law reports mention him no more. But the cause, despite mutations in its legal form, remained to be won, as if two glorious victories for freedom were of no avail. So once more the ceremonial was duly fulfilled and once more in a new litigious garb the Supreme Court met a familiar issue. This time it fell to Mr. Justice Roberts to announce that he was authorized to speak for the court in the celebrated cause of *Grovey* v. *Townsend*.[5] It is not usual for a judicial gratuity to be turned into "the opinion of the court" in the next case; but Roberts rose easily to this unorthodox feat. He forsook the world of reality; forgot that Texas is a one-party state and that exclusion from the Democratic primary meant complete denial of suffrage; converted the party into a private association; put the matter at issue completely outside

[4] The issue of "gratuitous judicial advice" has been discussed at some length before. The reader is warned not to condemn Mr. Justice Cardozo, who knew better than most judges that that sort of thing has no place in a judicial opinion, until the evidence is all in. The decision was reached by a vote of five to four; and here it is enough to call attention to the line-up. Concurring with Cardozo were Hughes, Brandeis, Stone, and Roberts; in dissent there were "the four horsemen," Van Devanter, McReynolds, Sutherland, and Butler. The fact of note is that, in a court otherwise evenly divided, Roberts cast the deciding vote.

[5] 295 U.S. 45; 313 U.S. 299; 319 U.S. 138. It is not without interest that Mr. Justice Roberts had concurred in the opinion of the Court in this case.

the political process. Thus having erected assumptions to his purpose, he had little trouble with his argument. Surely the gentlemen of a club are free to choose their own associates; the act of exclusion is neither directly nor by delegation the act of the state. So Grovey is stripped of his complaint—and his liberty—and is invited to leave the Court.

The startling fact, however, is that the report reveals no dissent. Yet the bench contained Hughes, a man so ingenious in "putting the question another way" and thus inducing his own answer as to be known as "the old fox"; Stone, whose feel for realism made him immune to neat crochet patches of legalism; Cardozo, first among his fellows in making the ancient law serve the felt needs of our times; and Brandeis, whose abiding passion was for social righteousness. It is not plausible to insist that such men were ignorant of modern political theory; that they believed that a state could act only through the formal agencies of government; that they were content to see substance of liberty fall before a legerdemain contrived to deny it. Nor can it be argued that they were caught without reasons with which to silence Roberts; dissenting opinions were quickly spread upon the pages of the liberal journals. Yet the fact—the unbelievable fact if you will—is that not one of this illustrious four made an attempt to answer back.

A victory of legalism over justice cannot, of course, endure; but for some years all was silent along the battle front. The state of Texas, whether as legislature or party convention, was well content to accept the Court's decision and the Negro voter was not easily induced once again to undertake a bout at law. At length the Supreme Court was induced to hear an appeal which was almost identical with that of *Grovey* v. *Townsend*. Reason and logic are changeless and neither statute nor by-law of party had undergone revision. But time had got in its dialectical licks and justices were now on the bench who knew the old cases only from the law books. So again on decision day, on another morning in May, Mr. Justice Reed announced, "I am authorized to speak for the Court in the case of *Smith* v. *Allwright*. He brushed away the idea that a political party is a gentleman's club; when all white citizens were eligible, and all of colored persuasion ineligible, it was a "mockery" to call it a "voluntary association." Between the decisions, a case with the strange caption of *U.S.* v. *Classic* has intervened; and to strike at political corruption in Louisiana, the Court had reversed the Newberry judgment. Reed then had little bother in making the primary and the election aspects of a common political process. It was easy, too, to find the act of the Democracy of Texas to be the act of the state. And a distinction between the executive committee and the state convention was too slight a difference upon which to rest the liberty of the citizen. *Grovey* v. *Townsend* was set aside and the Court brought its political theory up-to-date.

And so said all the justices[6]—except Mr. Justice Roberts. His dissent, that of an outraged man, brought other issues into the case. A more scolding indictment of the frailties of his brethren it is hard to find in all the United States reports. The judgment had come from justices who "deemed that they had a new light on the subject." They had assumed that a "knowledge and wisdom" resided in them which had been "denied to their predecessors." Nor could he forbear to remind them that such illustrious jurists as Hughes, Brandeis, and Cardozo had gone along when he had spoken in the Grovey case.[7] Such conduct on their part—he put on parade a number of horrible examples—was bringing into the law "an era of doubt and confusion." Its departures were creating hazards to "the stability of our institution." In a word, a Supreme Court decision had become a "restricted railroad ticket good for this day and trip only."

Opinions are circulated and revised in the light of criticism before delivery. Mr. Justice Reed was thus forced "in the opinion of the Court" to take account of the Roberts criticism before the dissent was voiced. Very quietly and for the bench he refused to impose upon the future the mistakes of the past. The Court, he insisted, "when convinced of former error was not contented to follow precedent." So, as precedents for a refusal to vest error, he lifted from a dissenting opinion of Brandeis a list of reversals and made it canoni-

[6] Mr. Justice Frankfurter, without opinion, concurred in the result.

[7] The thrust at Stone is pointed; for Stone alone among the justices now (1945) sitting had concurred in Roberts' opinion in *Grovey* v. *Townsend*.

cal by setting it down in the opinion of the court. Then, by citing later examples, he brought the imposing catalogue up to date. Where Roberts discovered only confusion, he saw trial and error as a weapon of probing injury.

The Roberts dissent, however, served an office which probably he did not intend. It is rare that the Court reveals what has gone on as it were backstage; and here, in a most illuminating way, the curtain is torn away and the mysteries of the former cases are cleared up. It is human, perhaps, that Roberts had a craftsman's pride in his decision of the Grovey case; and jurists, like other men of letters, are animated by a vested interest in their literary property. But here pride of authorship rises high above other values. Its object is not so much his opinion as his proprietorship in the neat distinction between the execution committee and the state convention as the source of the prohibition. That distinction appears first in Cardozo's opinion in *Nixon* v. *Corden*; yet it is alien to the idiom of Cardozo who, no more than Reed, would have put a human right at the mercy of a mere dialectical trick. It now appears that with the bench otherwise evenly divided, the court would go as Roberts voted. The writing of the distinction in that opinion—the gratuitous advice to the Democrats of Texas as to how the trick could be pulled off—was the price of his concurrence. When Texas followed instructions and the issue came back, what had gone before made Roberts the inevitable spokesman for the court. And just as inevitably a bargain between gentlemen, which was perhaps too subtle ever to find articulate expression, condemned Hughes, Brandeis, Cardozo, and Stone to silence. Thus an extremely vulnerable opinion drew no protest from a group of jurists who were artists at dissent. Thus a neat verbal trick of a single justice for years arrested and came very close to betraying a basic human right

The purpose here is to tell a story, not to preach a sermon. The story, however, would not be worth telling unless it had a meaning which ran far beyond its context. The hearsay of this article is a poor substitute for the direct evidence in the United States reports; and every person who values tolerance needs to discover from the opinions themselves the hazards to personal liberty which lurk within the intellectual folkways of men of good will. A legalist, not a lawyer, will discourse at length upon the technical differences between the four cases cited. But such tricks are of the mind of man. The fact, the inescapable fact, is that in all four cases exactly the same human right was in exactly the same danger. Nixon, Grovey, Lonnie Smith were, one and all, attempting to exercise the citizen's right to the ballot box at the only place in Texas where a vote could be made to count. Upon this plane of reality, it was the Roberts opinion which brought doubt and confusion into the law. Once the Supreme Court was led astray; once it stumbled in reaching a correct result; twice it came through clearly with a ringing judgment. But, after all, when the wisdom and knowledge of the highest court in the land is not always proof against its own verbal magic, can we really think of our civil rights as secure?

XII

WHAT WE ALL CAN DO

BY

R. M. MacIVER

In this concluding talk I am not going to try to distill the wisdom of all the talks you have listened to in this series. I have been impressed by the amount of wise and deep-probing guidance that they offer us on this subject of the relations of group to group. I hope that the contributions they have made will become a part of the armory of all who are engaged in this campaign, who are seeking for better relations between all groups in this country.

At the outset I want to express my own thanks and that of the Institute to those men who have addressed us here in this course. Most of them are engaged in exacting and engrossing affairs. In spite of that, they have sacrificed their convenience and their time in order to come and present their story to us. We are deeply indebted to them for the service they have rendered.

We who have been privileged to hear them speak here must have been stirred to ask the question: What can we, then, do about it?

Of course, to begin with, we all belong to organizations of one kind or another. Many of us belong to many organizations. Sometimes we do not even know how many we belong to. We can all use our influence in these organizations so that they shall not take actions that will involve discrimination or overt prejudice against their fellows.

We all have the opportunity to do something. Our organizations are different and our situations with respect to them are different. But I want rather to speak about what we can do individually in our daily life and practice, remembering that it is from the activity of many foci of influence that great movements grow and succeed. We can all of us be these foci of influence.

I want to talk very simply about certain things that we can do and, first of all, about our attitudes with respect to these things, for what we do depends on our attitudes. I want to consider how we should approach this subject, how we should carry into practice as individuals, as citizens, as members of families, as members of communities, the attitudes which are appropriate to our times and to our needs.

Let us remember first and foremost that the trouble we are concerned with does not depend on the differences between groups. It is not because different groups have different ways of life, different faiths, different opinions, different interests and different tastes—it is not because of diversity that we are in trouble and that our civilization is today in trouble. The problem is not how to cancel these differences. That belongs to the dead past. The problem is how to get along with these differences.

Nor are we seeking to end disagreements, to stop people from quarreling. Men love an honest fight, and I am all in favor of their having it. We are not seeking to discourage honest quarrels but only dishonest ones.

We are not seeking uniformity and we are certainly not seeking co-ordination. We do not want simply agreement between groups or even within groups. What we want is that these disagreements, these differences shall not tangle and balk our co-operation in our common concerns. That is what is so hard for us to achieve. That is what the primitive mind can never grasp. That is what the primitives among us forever resist—the co-operation of differences. There is our objective, not the removal of differences.

Let us not try, in fact, to conceal our differences. Let us accept them. This is not a neutral universe but an endlessly varied one, with all kinds of differences, new and old, forever appearing. Some things belong together and some things stay apart. Let them. We are not looking for any sweet repose of the lion and the lamb. We are not seeking for anything Utopian. We are seeking for something quite practical.

Therefore, let us stand by our differences. Let us not pretend, for example, that the other people are as right as we are, as our group is. How could they be? Let us admit the fact! But let us at the same time recognize that they have as much right to be wrong as we have —finish the sentence your own way.

And we are not seeking for merely a kindly tolerance. We are certainly not seeking for any kind of merely complacent or patronizing indifference.

Let us remember that we do not and did not make the universe— the universe that contains all our differences. Let us remember that we do not understand the universe that contains us all and all the other differences. We do not constitute the universe.

Remember the saying of the well-known author to a lady who said to him, thinking she was saying something bright when he asked her what she believed in. She said, "I accept the universe." And he replied, "Madam, you had better!"

All our tyrannies, all our little intolerances, all our prejudices against others, are our petty wilful ways of refusing to accept the universe. Let us accept it first, including its differences.

We tend to strut in our own little cave and think it is the cosmos. We humans are curious creatures. We are very wonderful; we are also very pathetic. We are never so pathetic as when we stand on stilts above others and hold up our chins, while our feet are staggering. That is what we do when we elevate ourselves above others.

Our little circle is no longer society. No one group any longer is the community. We have a bigger and a better world to live in than that, and it is good for us that it is so, provided we recognize it.

It is good for us, because then we have to defend with its own weapons our proper faiths, our opinions, our values. We have to defend them in a world in which other values and other faiths also exist. That is the only way in which they can be properly defended, and that is the only way in which they can show their worth.

The group has now to do, in fact, what the socially adult person always has had to do. Just as the person has to make his way with give-and-take, without diminution of his personality among other men, so now the group has to do among other groups. It has to live with other groups, as persons have to live with other persons.

That is a fact we have not realized yet; that is a condition of the kind of many-group society we now inhabit.

We have to co-operate with other groups, just as a person has to co-operate with other persons—to co-operate while still cherishing our own values. And remember, the basis of co-operation is that the common things, the things we share with others, the more inclusive things, are themselves the foundation of all our relations and that which makes possible the existence of all our differences.

That is the better, richer world we could enjoy. That is the world we shall enjoy in so far as we get rid of the narrow, little intolerances that separate group from group today.

To achieve that, we have to control the primitive in us. We have to control the primitives among us. They are the people who will not accept the universe. They are the people who shut themselves up in these little caves, who enclose their world with their own narrow walls. Then they cry out, "No doubt we are the people and wisdom will die with us."

How, then, can we be true to ourselves, our group selves? How can we be faithful to our values and still make one community?

First and foremost, I suggest by trusting our faiths. I mean that we trust them and do not try to support them by unworthy means; that we do not try to support them by petty bullying or petty discriminations; that we do not try to support them by denying the rights of others, as if that were any aid to the things we accept and believe.

We do not, in supporting our own faiths, belittle the humanity of other men. Let us not deny to other groups God's universe or our one community. Let us try to be fair-minded. We disapprove of the individual who seeks to bend others to his will, to his service. And so we should disapprove the conduct of groups who try to bend other groups to their exclusive will.

Always, in so far as I have spoken about group relations, I have tried to insist that the primary thing is the attitude back of our behavior; that the first need is to cultivate right attitudes; that our attitudes are based on understanding of our society; and that we carry, then, these attitudes through into wholesome practice.

I want to suggest some things we all can do, and some things we should not do. Let us not, for example, stick our angles into other men's sides. Minority groups do that no less than majority groups. They do it in many ways.

Take one example only. When a group forbids its children to associate with the children of other groups, they are doing that kind of thing. The offended offend in turn, and small rifts lead to large rifts. Exclusiveness breeds exclusiveness in turn, and from that other evils follow.

Now, there is here a problem that concerns religious groups. They have to respect the value in their religion that sets them apart; but they have got to avoid the unnecessary sequel of that necessity in the spirit of exclusiveness toward the community.

It is a difficult thing fully to deal with in a few words, but somehow they must compensate for their particular apartness by a greater inclusiveness in the whole community.

Which means, for example, that in matters that concern the whole community we should not think as members of our group, but as members of the community. It means that in all things we should practice meeting persons as they are, not as members of a group, of my group or of yours.

Otherwise, the group mind becomes a dangerous one. Otherwise the group mind becomes only one step from the mass mind, and the mass mind is primitive. The mass mind is blind. It is the enemy of all groups. If we let the mass mind get hold of us, it depersonalizes us, stampedes us; and we must train ourselves not to be stampeded.

Let us not follow the mass mind by saying that the members of some other group are all alike, all of the same cut and pattern, so that we can comfortably describe them in the same way. Let us not begin by thinking that all of this group are so-and-so's. If we do, then we shall conclude, when we meet somebody who belongs to this group, that he also is a so-and-so. If by any chance we meet somebody of the group who *is* a so-and-so, that confirms our social wisdom; that shows we were right all along. But if there are twenty others who do not appear to be so-and-so's, that merely means they are disguising the fact and we are still right! One favorable example proves us right. One hundred unfavorable examples do not prove us wrong. We have it both ways.

Let us be willing, again, to hear the arguments of the other side. Even though we know they are wrong, let us be patient enough to hear what they have got to say for themselves. If we will not listen to them, not only shall we not know what they stand for, but in effect we are dismissing them from our world. If we will not listen to them, it usually means we either fear or despise them, and both of these attitudes cut them out of our world.

There is something here for which we should envy the ways of children. Usually, until we spoil them, children have remarkable assurance in meeting others—up to a certain age, I mean. At this stage they combine frank curiosity with an unconscious assurance of themselves. We might envy that beautiful assurance of children.

Above all, we should not puff up our egos with pride because we are different from the other fellow. We should recognize that it is rather a mean way to exalt ourselves by debasing others. It is a very common refuge for men to exalt their own pride by claiming that they are better than others.

That spirit lies back of a good deal of discrimination, because, when we discriminate, it shows how much more fit we are. If we discriminate against another group, then, of course, we are superior; we are the elite. And you know what comfort that gives to us all.

For the same reason we should be chary about chuckling over the comic stories about other groups which show up their foibles or faults. That is a way in which we indulge our superiority and our pride, and it is also a way in which we tend to dismiss the other group from the community.

Of course, there are certain limits to this advice I am giving to you. It depends partly on the group. But when a group is in any way subject to the danger of discrimination or to the fact of discrimination, then to indulge in comic caricature of the group is a dangerous and unworthy thing that we should reject.

As I say, there are limits to it. For example, they tell a lot of comic tales about the way in which the Scotsman loves the penny and loves the bottle; but I would not worry about that because, you see, Scottish people are so self-assured they do not know when they are being made fun of! Besides, according to common repute, they do not understand a joke when they hear one!

Anyhow, let us show that we feel it is an insult, an insult to God and man, when someone dismisses another group with a contemptuous epithet. There are epithets of this sort that practically every group uses against every other group. There are epithets that make up for a lack of meaning by a fullness of derision.

Once more and finally, let us not passively accept actions of discrimination or prejudice practiced by those with whom we are associated, and particularly by the organizations to which we belong. Let us not think that it means nothing to us if a body to which we belong displays this spirit. It may be a club, or it may be a business group, or it may even be a church. Let us oppose it all we can. Let us make our own protest heard in the clearest possible way. And if we cannot make our protest felt in any other way, let us resign.

Need I go on? For all I am saying is that if we cultivate the right attitudes, then we cannot help carrying these into practices that will be daily serviceable to our cause. If we realize our community with other groups, we shall find daily opportunities to show it in practice. If we accept these opportunities, then we are united in the living faith that makes us more truly than any other way citizens—citizens of a country that first proclaimed this faith to the world. And that proclamation was never needed more than it is today.

CONTRIBUTORS TO
"UNITY AND DIFFERENCE IN AMERICAN LIFE"

EDWARD L. BERNAYS, B.S., *Cornell University,* public relations counsel to government, industries, corporations, other organizations; Author: *Propaganda, Crystallizing Public Opinion, Speak Up for Democracy, Take Your Place at the Peace Table.*

LOUIS FINKELSTEIN, Ph.D., *Columbia University;* Rabbi, *Jewish Theological Seminary of America;* President and Solomon Schechter Professor of Theology, Jewish Theological Seminary of America; Director, Institute for Religious and Social Studies; President, Conference on Science, Philosophy and Religion; Author: *Akiba, The Pharisees;* Co-editor: Symposia of Conference on Science, Philosophy and Religion.

LAWRENCE K. FRANK, A.B., *Columbia University,* Director, Caroline Zachry Institute of Human Development; Chairman, National Conference on Family Relations: Chairman, Committee on Food Habits, National Research Council; Contributor to professional journals, Lecturer.

E. FRANKLIN FRAZIER, Ph.D., *University of Chicago;* Professor and Head of Department of Sociology, Howard University; Member, American Sociological Society; Author: *The Negro Family in United States* (Anisfield award for best book in field of race relations, 1939), *Negro Youth at the Crossways, The Negro Family in Chicago.*

ELI GINZBERG, Ph.D., *Columbia University;* Director, Resources Analysis Division, Officer of the Surgeon General, War Department; Assistant Professor of Economics, School of Business, Columbia University; Contributor to economic journals; Author: *House of Adam Smith, Illusion of Economic Stability, Grass on the Slag Heaps, The Unemployed.*

WALTON H. HAMILTON, Ph.D., *University of Michigan;* Professor of Law, School of Law, Yale University; Author: *Price and Price Policies, The Pattern of Competition, Patents and Free Enterprise;* Co-author: *The Power to Govern, Anti-trust in Action;* Contributor to legal and economic periodicals.

GERALD W. JOHNSON, Litt.D., *Wake Forest;* LL.D., *Charleston,* North Carolina and D.C.L., *South;* Newspaperman; Editorial writer, Baltimore Evening Sun; Author: *The Wasted Land, America's Silver Age, Roosevelt: Dictator or Democrat?, American Heroes and Hero-Worship, An Honorable Titan,* etc.

R. M. MacIVER, D.Phil., *Edinburgh,* D.Litt., *Columbia, Harvard;* Lieber Professor of Political Philosophy and Sociology, Barnard College and Columbia University: Member, Fellowship Committee, Institute for Religious and Social Studies; Member, Board of Directors, Conference on Science, Philosophy and Religion; Author: *Community—A Sociological Study, The Modern State, Society—Its Structure and Changes, Leviathan and the People, Social Causation, Toward an Abiding Peace, The Web of Government;* Editor, *Group Relations and Group Antagonisms, Civilization and Group Relationships.* Co-editor: Symposia of Conference on Science, Philosophy and Religion.

CLYDE R. MILLER, E.D., *American International;* Associate Professor of Education, Teachers College, Columbia University; Founder, Institute for Propaganda Analysis, Inc.; League for Fair Play; Member, race relations committee, Federal Council of Churches; Consultant, Springfield, Massachusetts, public schools on educational program dealing with racial, religious and economic prejudices; Author: *The Process of Persuasion* and other works on public opinion.

ALLAN NEVINS, LL.D., *Washington and Lee, Miami;* Litt.D., *Dartmouth, Union;* Professor of American History, Columbia University; Member, National Institute of Arts and Letters, Council on Foreign Relations: Honorable fellow, N.Y. State Hist. Assn.; Author: *The Emergence of Modern America, Grover Cleveland—A Study in Courage* (Pulitzer Prize for best biography of year, 1932), *Hamilton Fish—The Inner History of the Grant Administration* (Pulitzer Prize, 1936), *America—The Story of a Free People;* General editor of the American Political Leaders Series, Yale Press Chronicles of America, new series.

RALPH W. SOCKMAN, LL.D., *Dickinson;* D.D., *Ohio Wesleyan;* Minister, Christ Church; Chairman, World Peace Committee, Methodist Church; Director, Union Theological Seminary, New York University, New York Medical College, Drew University; Trustee, Ohio Wesleyan; Minister of the National Radio Pulpit; Member, Harvard Board of Overseers; Chaplain, New York University; Author: *Recoveries of Religion, Life for Tomorrow, The Highway of God, Date with Destiny, Now to Live.*

VILHJALMUR STEFANSSON, Ph.D., LL.D., D.Litt., Explorer of lands and seas in Canadian and Alaskan sectors of the Arctic; Adviser on northern operations, Pan-American Airways; Contributor to popular and scientific magazines, technical publications of Canadian government and American Museum of Natural History; President, History of Science Society; Author of nineteen books, among them the *Northward Course of Empire, Ultima Thule, Greenland, Not by Bread Alone, The Friendly Arctic.*

INDEX

Adams, Charles Francis, 44
Adams, James Truslow, 18
Adler, Cyrus, 9
Africa, racial problem in, 43
Agar, Harold, 92-93
agriculture, distribution influenced by, 81
Alaska, and the ethnic issue, 62, 63, 65, 66, 67, 70
Alland, Alexander, 107n
America. *See* Latin America; North America; United States
American, as inaccurate title, 68-70
American Commonwealth (Bryce), 28
American culture, rise of, 15-31
American Federation of Labor, and the Negro, 54
American Indians, 43, 61-63, 72-73, 74
American Management Association, 142
American Revolution, 24
Asia, racial problem in, 43
assimilation, barriers to, 44, 50-59
Athenian society, 17
attitudes, importance of, 152-157
Australia, national character of, 17-18, 24

Baltimore, Md., newspaper of, 129
Barbeau, Marius, 74
Bernays, Edward L., lecture by, 131-142
Bill of Rights, 24, 25
biracial organization, theory of, 47-50, 58-59
Boas, Franz, 94
Brandeis, Louis D., 146n, 147, 148, 149
Britain. *See* Great Britain
Bryce, James, 19, 28
Bryson, Lyman, 9
business, and the race problem, 131-142. *See also* industry
Butler, Pierce, 146n

Canada: and the ethnic issue, 63, 65, 66, 67; and name "America," 68-69; national character of, 17
Cardoza, Benjamin N., 145-146, 146n, 147, 148, 149
Carr, Professor, 115
Challenge and Response, law of, 15
Charleston, S.C., toleration in, 25
Chatto, Clarence, 107n
Cherne, Leo, 109, 111
Chicago, Ill.: newspapers of, 127, 129; race riot in, 52
Chicago Sun, 127, 129
Chicago Tribune, 127
children, as minority groups, 35-36
Christianity, 115
churches, disunity of, 101-102
Churchill, Winston, 16
Cincinnati, Ohio, education for unity in, 114
civil rights: and the Negro, 46, 47, 49, 55-58, 137; shaping of American character by, 25, 26; in the Supreme Court, 143-150
Civil War, 23, 45
civilization, rise and decline of, 15
Civilization and Group Relationships (Conference), 3
class superiority, 110, 115, 116
Clemens, Samuel. *See* Twain, Mark
Collier, John, 63, 138
Columbus, Christopher, 63
Columbus, Ohio, education for unity in, 113, 114
columnists, newspaper, 124, 128
Committee on Recent Economic Changes, 26-27
common ground, of groups, 3-40
communication, channels of, 117, 131-132

community education, 113-118
conditioned responses, 108-110
Conference on Science, Philosophy, and Religion, 9
Congress of Industrial Organizations, 54, 141
Constitution, U.S., 24, 25, 122, 144-146
Corn Laws, 24
courts, role for unity, 143-150
culture, American, 15-31

Dana, Charles A., 128
Debs, Eugene V., 30
democracy: social order in, 33-34, 38-40; study of, 114-115
Democratic Party, 30-31
Denmark, treatment of Eskimos by, 63-65, 66
depression of 1930, 28-29, 79-80
Detroit race riot, 133, 139
differences, cooperation of, 152-157
discrimination, 48-49, 53-57, 86, 116, 135, 136, 138-139, 141-142, 151, 156-157
distribution, problem of, 78, 80-82, 83, 85, 116

economic insecurity, 92-93, 134
economic issue, in group conflict, 77-87
editorial expression, 124, 126-127, 129-130
education: community, 97-99, 113-118; in economic problems, 84; of Eskimos, 64-65, 66; and group tension, 90-91, 100, 136-137; for the Negro, 46, 48, 49; race tensions in, 134
Egede, Hans, 72
Eggleston, Edward, 22
England. See Great Britain
equality: of human needs, 39; shaping of American character by, 24-25, 26, 27; in the Soviet Union, 67-68
Eskimos, ethnic issue of, 63-67, 70-75
ethnic issue, in group conflict, 61-75
Europe, origin of racial problem in, 43
European civilization, influence on America of, 19

Fair Employment Practice Committee, 53-54, 116

fear, as source of tension, 92-93, 134
Federal Council of Churches of Christ in America, 136, 141
Federal government: control by, 28-31, 79-80, 86, 87; and the race problem, 138-139
Federal Housing Authority, 53
Field, Marshall, 127
Fifteenth Amendment, 144
Fine, Benjamin, 107n
Finkelstein, Louis, 3, 9; lecture by, 5-13
Fiske, John, 16
Folkways (Sumner), 109
foreign economic relations, 78, 82-83, 84, 85
Fortas, Abe, 138
Fourteenth Amendment, 144-145
France: Canadian rule of, 17; national character of, 16, 24
Francis of Assisi, St., 95
Frank, Lawrence K., chapter by, 3-40
Frankfurter, Felix, 148n
Frazier, E. Franklin, lecture by, 43-59
free enterprise, shaping of American character by, 21-23, 26, 27, 30
freedom of the press, 122-123, 126
freedoms, achievement of, 35
frontier, shaping of American character by, 19-20
Frost, Robert, 98

Gallup Poll, 127, 128, 129
Garvey Movement, 55
George, David Lloyd, 30
Germany: and control of trade, 86; and mass phobia, 109, 110, 117; national character of, 16, 23, 24, 25
Ginzberg, Eli, lecture by, 77-87
Godkin, Edwin L., 19
Gompers, Samuel, 30
government control, 28-31, 79-80, 86, 87
Granger Laws, 24
Great Britain: colonies of, 17, 21, 23-24, 25; and control of trade, 86; influence on Americans of, 18; national character of, 16, 23, 24, 30
Greeley, Horace, 128

Greenland, and the ethnic issue, 63-65, 66, 70, 72
group relations: and the common good, 5-13; series of addresses on, 3
Group Relations and Group Antagonisms (Conference), 3
group tensions: in changing social order, 37-38; immunization against, 108-111, 112, 117; and prejudice, 89-96; visibility of, 131. *See also* groups
groups: cooperation needed for, 152-157; ethnic, 61-75; and national unity, 3-13; racial, 43-59, 131-142; religious, 89-104; in social order, 34-40
Grovey v. *Townsend,* 146-148, 149

Halligan, Alice, 107n
Hamilton, Alexander, 122
Hamilton, Walton Hale, lecture by, 143-150
Harlem schools, 112-113, 137
Harte, Bret, 22
Hartill, Dr., 112
Harvard University, 96
Hegel, Georg W. F., 19
Hezekiah, 9
Hill, Frank E., 18
history, distortion of, 101
History of the Warfare of Science with Theology (White), 109
Hitler, Adolph, 63
Holmes, Oliver W., 143-145
Hoover, Herbert, 26, 28, 30
housing, in race relations, 52-53
Hughes, Charles Evans, 144, 146n, 147, 148, 149
humilities, need for, 93-95
Hunter College, 91
Huxley, Thomas H., 94-95

Ickes, Harold, 62, 138
ignorance, as source of prejudice, 90, 102
immigration, shaping of American character by, 20-21, 30
imperialism, 82
Indians. *See* American Indians; Eskimos

individual: attitudes of, 151-157; status of, 33-40
individualism, shaping of American character by, 23-24, 26-27, 30
indoctrination, 91, 98-99, 102-103, 104
industrial revolution, in the U.S., 21-23
industry: and the Negro, 50, 53-55, 109; and newspapers, 120-122; race tensions in, 134. *See also* business
insecurity, 37-38, 92-93, 134
Institute for Religious Studies, 3
intermarriage, 58
Interstate Commerce Act, 24
investment bankers, and the race problem, 140, 142
Ives-Quinn Anti-Discrimination Bill, 139

Jackson, Andrew, 24, 29
Japan, and mass phobia, 109, 110
Jefferson, Thomas, 24, 29, 122, 125
Jewish Theological Seminary of America, 9-10
"John Bull's Other Island" (Shaw), 26
Johnson, F. Ernest, 9
Johnson, Gerald W., lecture by, 119-130
Johnson, James Weldon, 135
Johnson, Tom, 30
Jones, Golden Rule, 30
journalism, personal, 128
Judaism, 115
judiciary, 143-150
Julius Rosenwald Fund, 134, 135
Jungle, The (Sinclair), 22

Kingsley, Charles, 94

labor, race tensions in, 134
labor unions: distribution influenced by, 81; and the Negro, 54-55, 141-142
language, Eskimo, 70-72
Latin America, and name "America," 68-69, 70
League for Fair Play, 107n
Lincoln, Abraham, 29
Lindeman, Professor, 96
Lippmann, Walter, 29, 128
literature, Eskimo, 70-72

London Economic Conference, 82

long-range planning, in group relations, 5, 7-10, 12-13

Louis XIV, 17

Lowell, A. Lawrence, 96-97

MacIver, R. M., 9, 68, 92, 103-104, 135; lecture by, 151-157

McReynolds, Jas. C., 146n

Magyar language, 72

Maryland, toleration in, 25

Marx, Karl, 77

mass phobias, 108-110, 117-118, 155

Maxwell, Elsa, 108

mercantilism, rebellion against, 23-24

Miller, Clyde R., 107n; lecture by, 107-118

minority groups, 35-38. *See also* groups

monopoly, newspaper, 123-124, 126, 129-130

Morais, Sabato, 9

morals, in economic problems, 83-84

Mowrer, Edgar Ansell, 63

Munsterberg, Hugo, 26

Murray, J. Edgar, 107-108

Murray, Philip, 141

Napoleon III, 24

National Association for the Advancement of Colored People, 135

national character, formation of, 15-31

National City Bank of New York, bulletin of, 116

National Conference of Christians and Jews, 96

national cultures, rise and decline of, 15

National Labor Relations Act, 54

National Negro Business League, 48

National Socialism, 16

national unity. *See* unity

nationality, nomenclature of, 68-70

"Nature of Race Relations, The" (Park), 44n

Negroes: business approach to problem of, 135-142; civil rights cases for, 143-150; in industry, 50, 53-55, 109; propaganda

for, 100-101, 103; as a racial problem, 43-59; war tension of, 132-134

Nevins, Allan, lecture by, 15-31

New Deal, 28, 80

New York (State), civil rights in, 137

New York, N.Y.: newspapers of, 129; toleration in, 25

New York Herald-Tribune, 62-63, 128

New York Mayor's Committee on Unity, 138

New York Post, 63, 108

New York Sun, 128

New York Times, 96, 127

New York Tribune, 128

New York World Telegram, 112-113

New Zealand, national character of, 17-18, 24, 30

Newark, N.J., education for unity in, 113, 114

Newport, R.I., toleration in, 25

newspapers: Negro, 46-47; and race tensions, 131, 132. *See also* press

Nixon v. Condon, case of, 145-146, 149

Nixon v. Herndon, case of, 143-145

North America, British colonies of, 17, 21, 23-24, 25

Noyes, Alfred, 91

optimism, shaping of American character by, 26-27

Oriental, as a racial problem, 44

Ovington, Mary White, 135

Park, Robert E., 44n

Parkman, Francis, 17

Penn, William, 25

Pennsylvania, toleration in, 25

Philippines, and the ethnic issue, 69

physical characteristics, Negro, 50-51

Pittsburgh, Pa., education for unity in, 113, 114, 117n

PM, 128-129

Political Action Committee, 141

population-income pyramid, 80-81

prejudice, 89-96, 102, 151, 153, 157; immunization against, 112-118

press, role for unity, 119-130. *See also* newspapers
pride, 93-95, 156
Process of Persuasion, The (Miller), 107n
production, problems of, 78, 79-80, 83, 116
professions, and race problems, 137
propaganda, effective, 96-97, 99, 101
protection *v.* free trade, 86
public opinion: and the Gallup Poll, 127; newspapers as molders of, 121, 126-130; and visibility, 131

race, nomenclature of, 68-70
race relations: and business, 139-142; and the courts, 143-150; index of, 134
race riots, 131-132, 133, 139
racial groups, 43-59, 131-142. *See also* Negroes
racial issue, division by, 43-59
racial superiority, 93-94, 110, 113, 115, 116, 117
racial tensions: accentuated by war, 132-134; low visibility of, 131
radio: effect on newspapers of, 130; and the racial problem, 132
Reconstruction Finance Corporation, 30
Reconstruction Period, 45-46, 56
Reed, Stanley F., 147-149
regimentation, 34-37; wartime, 30
religion: Eskimo, 74-75; and the race problem, 135-136, 141
religious groups, 155
religious issue, division by, 89-104
religious superiority, 110, 115, 116
religious tensions, low visibility of, 131
Renan, Ernest, 16
Republican Party, 30-31, 45-46
Rest of Your Life, The (Cherne), 109
Rhode Island, toleration in, 25
Riis, Jacob, 30
Roberts, Owen J., 146, 146n, 147, 148-149, 150
Romulo, General, 69
Roosevelt, Franklin D., 28, 29, 30, 80, 120-121, 127
Roosevelt, Theodore, 29, 30

Russia, national character of, 16. *See also* Soviet Union

Sandburg, Carl, 22
scarcity, delusion of, 110, 115-116
Schechter, Solomon, 9
schools, unity through, 107-118. *See also* education
science, in human relationships, 116-117
scientific weapons, for unity, 4
Seddon, King Dick, 30
segregation, Negro, 52-53, 56-57
Shaw, George Bernard, 26
Sherman Anti-Trust Act, 24
Shintoism, 110
Shuster, George N., 91, 98, 100
Siberia, and the ethnic issue, 63
Simon, Jules, 97
Sinclair, Upton, 22
slavery, in the South, 44-45
Smith, Adam, 24, 79, 82, 84
Smith v. *Allwright,* case of, 147-148
social cooperation, and the American character, 27-31
social inheritance, as source of prejudice, 90, 102
social order, maintenance of, 33-40
social philosophy, in economic problems, 84-85
social workers, and the race problem, 135
Sockman, Ralph W., lecture by, 89-104
South, race relations in, 44-46, 48-49, 56-58
Soviet Union: racial groups of, 66-68, 70, 75; treatment of Eskimos by, 63, 66-68. *See also* Russia
Spargo, John, 30
Spartan society, 17
spiritual life, and group unity, 4, 5, 10-13
Springfield Plan, 97, 99, 113, 114, 117n; literature on, 107n
Springfield Plan—A Photographic Record (Alland and Wise), 107n
state: as interventionist, 28-31, 79-80, 86, 87; power of, 23-24
Stefansson, Vilhjalmur, lecture by, 61-75
Steffens, Lincoln, 30

Stone, Harlan F., 146n, 147, 148n, 149
Story of the Springfield Plan, The (Halligan and Chatto), 107n
Study of History, A (Toynbee), 15
suffrage: court decisions on right of, 143-150; for the Negro, 45, 47, 48, 56
superiority, 110-111, 112-118, 156
Supreme Court, and civil rights, 143-150
Sutherland, George, 146n
Sweden, national character of, 16
Switzerland, national character of, 16

Temple, Archbishop, 98, 102
tensions. *See* group tensions
Texas, and civil rights, 143-150
Thorndike, Lynn, 108
Time for Greatness (Agar), 92-93
Tocqueville, A. C. de, 26
Toynbee, Arnold, 15
Turner, Frederick J., 19
Twain, Mark, 22

unity: and business, 131-142; common ground of, 3-40; and the courts, 143-150; economic issue in, 77-87; ethnic issue in, 61-75; and the individual, 151-157; and the press, 119-130; racial issue in, 43-59; religious issue in, 89-104; and the schools, 107-118
United States: ethnic attitude in, 61-63, 65, 68, 69, 72-73; and group unity, 3-7; as a multigroup country, 75, 77-78; newspaper inconsistency in, 124-126;

racial problem in, 43-59; rise of culture in, 15-31
U.S. v. *Classic,* case of, 148
Uzbeks, 70

Van Devanter, Willis, 146n
veterans, as chauvinists, 85, 86-87
Villard, Oswald Garrison, 135
visibility, public opinion characterized by, 131, 135
voting. *See* suffrage

Wall Street Journal, 125
Wallace, Henry A., 138
war, economic interpretation of, 82
Washington, Booker T., 48
Wealth of Nations (Smith), 24, 79
West Indies, racial problem in, 43
White, Andrew Dickson, 109
Whitlock, Brand, 30
Williams, Roger, 25
Willkie, Wendell, 121
Wilson, Woodrow, 29
Wise, James Waterman, 107n
women, as minority groups, 35
world unity, 6-7
World War I, 27, 30; and the Negro, 46, 47, 55
World War II: foreign trade in, 86; and the Negro, 55, 59; and racial tensions, 132-134, 139
Writers' War Board, 132